# The Moosehead Anthology

A

COLLECTION OF CONTEMPORARY WRITING

EDITED BY

THE STAFF OF THE MOOSEHEAD REVIEW

LIVRES
DC
BOOKS

MONTREAL

EDITED by the staff of the Moosehead Review: Mona Adilman, Karen Haughian, Shirley MacGregor, Robert Majzels, Rowan Miles, Christopher O'Brien, Louis Olivenstein, Renée Salama, Emil Sher.

EDITOR-IN-CHIEF Robert Allen.

THE MOOSEHEAD ANTHOLOGY is published in Quebec by D.C. Books. Subscription rates are: single issues $6.95; two years $12.00; overseas $15.00 per issue; libraries $15.00; lifetime subscriptions $50.00. Subscriptions and manuscripts should be sent to: English Dept., Sir George Williams Campus, Concordia University, 1455 de Maisonneuve Blvd. West, Montreal, Quebec, H3B 1M8, Canada.

A public reading of "All Corpses Are Equal" was performed at the Playwrights' Workshop in March, 1986.

"The Guerilla is Like a Poet" by José Maria Sison was previously published in *Prison and Beyond* (Manila: Free José Ma. Sison Committee, 1984).

"Los Baños, Interlude I and II" was published in *Philippines Studies*, 33, 1985.

The Moosehead Anthology gratefully acknowledges the assistance of the English Department and the Graduate English Students' Association.

Book design and typesetting by Karen Haughian
Cover design and painting by Jerome Krause
Moosehead logo designed by Margaret Matson

Printed in Canada

ISBN 0-919688-00-4

# CONTENTS

## Sharing Poems With The Cat

The new book out and the only one here
to celebrate with me is the cat.
He's a smart cat alright, but he'd rather
have a fish tail or a full tin of beef
plopped in his dish. What better
eyes to take in the cover, though,
aloof and wise, their black disks
pulling everything inside. Somewhere
in his dark Egyptian brain, the blue
letters of the title will sit beside
his memory of a robin's sweet anatomy
and the precise, entirely cat-like genes
that make his metrics unsurpassable,
his caesuras dangerous to the dragonfly.
Oh, his oxymorons, the soft music of his paws,
the risks he takes with his daring and domestic
leap-to-the-edge-of-the-bathtub lines.

LORNA CROZIER

## Two Songs For Crickets

1.

Silence just before rain.
Then the clear
clairvoyant note of one cricket
drawing its thin bow
across my thought of it,
small and dark
in the dry grasses.


2.

Crickets begin
to build their house
out of night.

How many crickets
can live in one room,
play their dark violins
with their elbows out

till light breaks
their strings
one by one.

*Seasons*

I wish there were a season for mating
like with grouse or salmon (the Atlantic
kind that survives, adding ring after ring
to its scales.)
                    One time of year
you wanted it,
drumming or defying gravity,
and for the rest
you just went about your day.
A grouse folded in feathers,
a salmon moving its fine bones downstream.

Or being human, to fall asleep
late in the afternoon in a double bed,
naked or not, the body
busy with its own life, giving up
on love and beauty, words
like *hand shoulder inner thigh*
meaning simply what they say.

IRVING LAYTON

*Overman*

Knowing despair
and knowing that he knows
despair
how can a man despair?

Cognizing inhumanity
is mankind's distinguishing mark
inviolable by time or flux
the well-constituted man rejoices
and loves.

## Soft Porn

In the antique bowl
the apple's skin
glowed
rosy and fresh
like a young girl's

A July heatwave
brought the mottling
spots of decay

The lascivious assaults
of death:
love's pornographic twin

TODD SWIFT

*2/21/86*
for S.R.

Somewhere along the line of the last few
months I have loved you
like Florida land,
sight unseen, except for your pitch
over the eyeless wire in my ear
like a bug crawled in:
I feel it, hear it tapping,
but its description I imagine,
you have grown out your hair
until you are beautiful
and not so mousy,
and when I inch a finger
around your waist
I pinch thin perfection
you have grown into.

## Death of a Son

At last we got the body.

Wednesday. Just enough time for a Saturday funeral. We were exhausted. Empty. The funeral still ahead of us. We had to find the strength to grieve. There had been no time for grief, really. Only much bewilderment and confusion. Not grief. For isn't grief the awareness of loss?

That is why when we finally got the body, Buntu said: "Do you realize our son is dead?" I realized. Our awareness of the death of our first and only child had been displaced completely by the effort to get his body. Even the horrible events that caused the death: we did not think of them, as such. Instead, the numbing drift of things took over our minds: the pleas, letters to be written, telephone calls to be made, telegrams to be dispatched, lawyers to consult, "influential" people to "get in touch with," undertakers to be contacted, so much walking and driving. That is what suddenly mattered: the irksome details that blur the goal (no matter how terrible it is); each detail becoming a door which, once unlocked, revealed yet another door. Without being aware of it, we were distracted by the smell of the skunk and not by what the skunk had done.

We realized something too, Buntu and I, that during the two-week effort to get our son's body, we had drifted apart. For the first time in our marriage, our presence to each other had become a matter of habit. He was there. He'll be there. And I'll be there. But when Buntu said: "do you realize our son is dead," he uttered a thought that suddenly brought us together again. It was as if the return of the body of our son was also our coming together. For it was only at that moment that we really began to grieve; as if our lungs had suddenly begun to take in air when just before, we were beginning to suffocate. Something with meaning began to emerge.

We realized.

We realized that something else had been happening to us, adding to the terrible events. Yes, we had drifted apart. Yet, our estrangement, just at that moment when we should have been together, seemed disturbingly comforting to me. I was comforted in a manner I did not quite understand.

The problem was that I had known all along that we would have to buy the body anyway. I had known all along. Things would end that way. And when things turned out that way, Buntu could not look me in the eye. For he had said:

"Over my dead body! Over my dead body!"

as soon as we knew we would be required to pay the police or the government for the release of the body of our child.

"Over my dead body! Over my dead body!" Buntu kept on saying.

11

Finally, we bought the body. We have the receipt. The police insisted we take it. That way, they would be "protected". It's the law, they said.

I suppose we could have got the body earlier.

At first I was confused, for one is supposed to take comfort in the heroism of one's man. Yet, inwardly, I could draw no comfort from his outburst. It seemed hasty. What sense was there to it when all I wanted was the body of my child? What would happen if, as events unfolded, it became clear that Buntu would not give up his life? What would happen? What would happen to him? To me?

For the greater part of two weeks, all of Buntu's efforts, together with friends, relatives, lawyers and the newspapers, were to secure the release of the child's body without the humiliation of having to pay for it. A "fundamental principle".

Why was it difficult for me to see the wisdom of the principle? The worst thing, I suppose, was worrying about what the police may have been doing to the body of my child. How they may have been busy prying it open "to determine the cause of death".
Would I want to look at the body
when we finally got it? To see further mutilations in addition to the "cause of death"? What kind of mother would not want to look at the body of her child? People will ask. Some will say: "it's grief." She is too grief-stricken.
"But still. . . " they will say.
And the elderly among them may say: "young people are strange."
But how can they know?
It was not that I would not want to see the body of my child, but that I was too afraid to confront the horrors of my own imagination. I was haunted by the thought of how useless it had been to have created something. What had been the point of it all? This body filling up with a child. The child steadily growing into something that could be seen and felt. Moving, as it always did, at that time of day when I was all alone at home waiting for it. What had been the point of it all?
How can they know that the mutilation to determine "the cause of death" ripped my own body? Can they think of a womb feeling hunted? Disgorged?
And the milk that I still carried. What about it? What had been the point of it all?
Even Buntu did not seem to sense that that principle, the "fundamental principle", was something too intangible for me at that moment; something that I desperately wanted should assume the form of my child's body. He still seemed far from ever knowing.

12

I remember one Saturday morning
early in our courtship, as Buntu and I walked hand-in-hand through town,
window-shopping. We cannot even be said to have been window-shopping,
for we were aware of very little that was not ourselves. Everything in those
windows was merely an excuse for words to pass between us.
We came across three girls sitting on the pavement, sharing a packet of fish
and chips after they had just bought it from a nearby Portuguese cafe.
Buntu said: "I want fish and chips too." I said: "So seeing is desire." I
said: "My man is greedy!" We laughed. I still remember how he tightened
his grip on my hand. The strength of it!

Just then, two white boys coming in the opposite direction suddenly rushed
at the girls, and, without warning, one of them kicked the packet of fish and
chips out of the hands of the girl who was holding it. The second boy
kicked away the rest of what remained in the packet. The girl stood up
shaking her hand as if to throw off the pain in it. Then she pressed it under
her armpit as if to squeeze the pain out of it. Meanwhile, the two boys
went on their way laughing. The fish and chips lay scattered on the
pavement and on the street like stranded boats on a river that had gone dry.

"Just let them do that to you!"
said Buntu, tightening once more his grip on my hand as we passed on like
sheep that had seen many of their own in the flock picked out for slaughter.
We would note the event and wait for our turn. I remember I looked at
Buntu, and saw his face was somewhat glum. There seemed no connection
between that face and the words of reassurance just uttered. For a while, we
went on quietly. It was then that I noticed his grip had grown somewhat
limp. Somewhat reluctant. Having lost its self-assurance, it seemed to
have been holding on because it had to, not because of a confident sense of
possession.

It was not to be long before his words were tested. How could fate work
this way, giving to words meanings and intentions they did not carry when
they were uttered? I saw that day, how the language of love could so easily
be trampled underfoot, or scattered like fish and chips on the pavement, and
left stranded and abandoned like boats in a river that suddenly went dry.
Never again was love to be confirmed with words. The world around us was
too hostile for vows of love. At any moment, the vows could be subjected
to the stress of proof. And love died. For words of love need not be tested.
On that day,
Buntu and I began our silence. We talked and laughed, of course, but we
stopped short of words that would demand proof of action. Buntu knew. He
knew the vulnerability of words. And so, he sought to obliterate words
with acts that seemed to promise redemption.

13

On that day,
as we continued with our walk in town, that Saturday morning, coming up towards us from the opposite direction, was a burly Boer walking with his wife and two children. They approached Buntu and me with an ominously determined advance. Buntu attempted to pull me out of the way, but I never had a chance. The Boer shoved me out of the way, as if clearing a path for his family. I remember, I almost crashed into a nearby fashion display window. I remember, I glanced at the family walking away, the mother and the father each dragging a child. It was for one of those children that I had been cleared away. I remember, also, that as my tears came out, blurring the Boer family and everything else, I saw and felt deeply what was inside of me: a desire to be avenged.

But nothing happened.
All I heard was Buntu say: "The dog!"
At that very moment, I felt my own hurt vanish like a wisp of smoke. And as my hurt vanished, it was replaced, instead, by a tormenting desire to sacrifice myself for Buntu. Was it something about the powerlessness of the curse and the desperation with which it had been made? The filling of stunned silence with an utterance? Surely it ate into him, revealing how incapable he was of meeting the call of his words.

And so it was, that that afternoon, back in the township, left to ourselves at Buntu's home, I gave in to him for the first time. Or should I say I offered myself to him? Perhaps from some vague sense of wanting to heal something in him? Anyway, we were never to talk about that event. Never. We buried it alive deep inside of me that afternoon. Would it ever be exhumed? All I vaguely felt and knew was that I had the keys to the vault.

That was three years ago; a year before we married.
The cause of death?
One evening I returned home from work, particularly tired after I had been covering more shootings by the police in the East Rand. Then I had hurried back to the office in Johannesburg to piece together on my typewriter, the violent scenes of the day, and then to file in my report to meet the deadline. It was late when I returned home; and when I got there, I found a crowd of people in the yard. They were those who could not get inside. I panicked. What had happened? I did not ask those who were outside, being desperate to get into the house. They gave way easily when they recognized me.

Then I heard my mother's voice. Her cry rose well above the noise. It turned into a scream when she saw me. "What is it, mother?" I asked, embracing her out of a vaguely despairing sense of terror. But she pushed me away with a hysterical violence that astounded me.

"What misery have I brought you, my child?" she cried. At that point, many women in the room began to cry too. Soon, there was much wailing in the room, and then all over the house. The sound of it! The anguish! Understanding, yet eager for knowledge, I became desperate. I had to hold

14

on to something. The desire to embrace my mother no longer had anything to do with comforting her, for whatever she had done, whatever its magnitude, had become inconsequential. I needed to embrace her for all the anguish that tied everyone in the house into a knot. I wanted to be part of that knot, yet I wanted to know what had brought it about.

Eventually, we found each other, my mother and I, and clasped each other tightly. When I finally released her, I looked around at the neighbours and suddenly had a vision of how that anguish had to be turned into a simmering kind of indignation. The kind of indignation that had to be kept at bay only because there was a higher purpose at that moment: the sharing of concern.

Slowly, and with a calmness that surprised me, I began to gather the details of what had happened. Instinctively, I seemed to have been gathering notes for a news report.

It happened that during the day, the soldiers and the police who had been patrolling the township in their Casspirs began to shoot in the streets at random. Need I describe what I did not see? How did the child come to die just at that moment when the police and the soldiers began to shoot at random, at any house, at any moving thing? That was how one of our windows was shattered by a bullet. And that was when my mother, who looked after her grandchild when we were away at work, panicked. She picked up the child and ran to the neighbours. It was only when she entered the neighbour's house that she noticed the wetness of the blanket that covered the child she held to her chest, as she ran for the sanctuary of the neighbours. She had looked at her unaccountably bloody hand, then she noted the still bundle in her arms, and began at that moment to blame herself for the death of her grandchild. . .

Later,

the police, on yet another round of shooting, found people gathered at our house. They stormed in, saw what had happened. At first, they dragged my mother out, threatening to take her away unless she agreed not to say what had happened. But then they returned, and instead, took the body of the child away. By what freak of logic did they hope that by this act their carnage would never be discovered?

That evening,

I looked at Buntu closely. He appeared suddenly to have grown older. We stood alone in an embrace in our bedroom. I noticed, when I kissed his face, how his once lean face had grown suddenly puffy.

At that moment, I felt the familiar impulse come upon me once more; the impulse I always felt when I sensed that Buntu was in some kind of danger; the impulse to yield something of myself to him. He wore the look of someone struggling to gain control of something. Yet, it was clear he was far from controlling anything. I knew that look. Had seen it many times. It came at those times when I sensed that he faced a wave that was infinitely

15

NJABULO S. NDEBELE

stronger than he; that it would certainly sweep him away, but that he had to seem to be struggling. I pressed myself tightly to him as if to vanish into him, as if only the two of us could stand up to the wave.

"Don't worry," he said. "Don't worry. I'll do everything in my power to right this wrong. Everything. Even if it means suing the police." We went silent.

I knew that silence.

But I knew something else at that moment: that I had to find a way of disengaging myself from the embrace.

Suing the police?

I listened to Buntu outlining his plans. "Legal counsel. That's what we need," he said. "I know some people in Pretoria," he said. As he spoke, I felt the warmth of intimacy between us cooling. When he finished, it was cold. I disengaged from his embrace slowly, yet purposefully. Why had Buntu spoken?

Later, he was to speak again, when all his plans had failed to work:

"Over my dead body! Over my dead body!"

He sealed my lips. I would wait for him to feel and yield one day to all the realities of misfortune.

Ours was a home, it could be said.

It seemed a perfect life for a young couple: I, a reporter, Buntu, a personnel officer at an American factory manufacturing farming implements. He had travelled to the United States and returned with a mind fired with dreams. We dreamed together. Much time we spent, Buntu and I, trying to make a perfect home. The occasions are numerous on which we paged through *Femina, Fair Lady, Cosmopolitan, Home Garden, Car,* as if somehow we were going to surround our lives with the glossiness in the magazines. Indeed, much of our time was spent window-shopping through the magazines. This time, it was different from the window-shopping we did that Saturday when we courted. This time our minds were consumed by the things we saw and dreamed of owning: the furniture, the fridge, TV, video cassette recorders, washing machines, and even a vacuum cleaner, and every other imaginable thing that would ensure a comfortable modern life.

Especially when I was pregnant.

What is it that Buntu did not buy, then?

And when the boy was born, Buntu changed the car. A family, he would say, must travel comfortably.

The boy became the center of Buntu's life. Even before he was born, Buntu had already started making inquiries at white private schools. That was where he would send his son, the bearer of his name.

Dreams!

It is amazing how the horrible findings of my newspaper reports often vanished before the glossy magazines of our dreams; how I easily forgot that

16

the glossy images were concocted out of the keys of typewriters; made by writers whose business was to sell dreams at the very moment that death pervaded the land. So powerful are words and pictures that even their makers often believe in them.

Buntu's ordeal was long. So it seemed. He would get up early every morning to follow up the previous day's leads regarding the body of our son. I wanted to go with him, but each time I prepared to go, he would shake his head.

"It's my task," he would say.

But every evening he returned, empty-handed, while with each day that passed and we did not know where the body of my child was, I grew restive and hostile in a manner that gave me much pain. Yet Buntu always felt compelled to give a report on each day's events. I never asked for it. I suppose it was his way of dealing with my silence.

One day he would say: "The lawyers have issued a court order that the body be produced. The writ of *habeas corpus*."

On another day he would say: "We have petitioned the Minister of Justice."

On yet another he would say: "I was supposed to meet the Chief Security Officer. Waited the whole day. At the end of the day they said I would see him tomorrow if he was not going to be too busy. They are stalling."

Then he would say: "The newspapers, especially yours, are raising the hue and cry. The government is bound to be embarrassed. It's a matter of time."

And so it went on. Every morning he got up and left. Sometimes alone; sometimes with friends. He always left to bear the failure alone.

How much did I care about lawyers, petitions, and Chief Security Officers? A lot. The problem was that whenever Buntu spoke about his efforts, I heard only his words. I felt in him, the disguised hesitancy of someone who wanted reassurance without asking for it. I saw someone who got up every morning and left not to look for results, but to search for something he could only have found with me.

And each time he returned, I gave my speech to my eyes. And he answered without my having parted my lips. As a result, I sensed, for the first time in my life, a terrible power in me, that could make him do anything. And he would never ever be able to deal with that power as long as he did not silence my eyes and call for my voice.

And so, he had to prove himself.

And while he left each morning, I learned to be brutally silent. Could he prove himself without me? Could he? Then I got to know those days, what I'd always wanted from him. I got to know why I have always drawn him into me whenever I sensed his vulnerability.

I wanted him to be free to fear.

Wasn't there greater strength that way? Had he ever lived with his own feelings? And the stress of life in this land: didn't it call out for men to be

17

heroes? And should they live up to it even though the details of the war to be fought may often be blurred?

They should.

Yet it is precisely for that reason that I often found Buntu's thoughts lacking in strength. They lacked the experience of strife that could only come from a humbling acceptance of fear and then, only then, the need to fight it.

Me?

In a way, I have always been free to fear. The prerogative of being a girl. It was always expected of me to scream when a spider crawled across the ceiling. It was known I would jump onto a chair whenever a mouse blundered into the room.

Then, once more, the Casspirs came.

A few days before we got the body back, I was at home with my mother when we heard the great roar of truck engines. There was much running and shouting in the streets. I saw them, as I've always seen them on my assignments: the Casspirs. On five occasions they ran down our street at great speed, hurling tear gas canisters at random. On the fourth occasion, they got our house. The canister shattered another window and filled the house with the terrible pungent choking smoke that I had got to know so well. We ran out of the house gasping for fresh air.

So, this was how my child was killed?

Could they have been the same soldiers? Now hardened to their tasks? Or were they new ones being hardened to their tasks? Did they drive away laughing? Clearing paths for their families? What paths?

And was this our home?

It couldn't be. It had to be a little bird's nest waiting to be plundered by a predator bird. There seemed no sense to the wedding pictures on the walls; the graduation pictures; birthday pictures; pictures of relatives, and paintings of lush landscapes. There seemed no sense anymore to what seemed recognizably human in our house. It took only a random swoop to obliterate personal worth, to blot out any value there may have been to the past. In desperation, we began to live only for the moment. I do feel hunted.

It was on the night of the tear gas

that Buntu came home, saw what had happened, and broke down in tears. They had long been in the coming. . .

My own tears welled out too.

How much did we have to cry to refloat stranded boats? I was sure they would float again.

A few nights later, on the night of the funeral,

exhausted, I lay on my bed, listening to the last of the mourners leaving. Slowly, I became conscious of returning to the world. Something came back after it seemed not to have been there for ages. It came as a surprise, as a reminder that we will always live around what will happen. The sun will rise and set, and the ants will do their endless work, until one day the clouds turn grey and rain falls, and that even in the township, the ants will fly out into the sky. Come what may.

My moon came,

in a heavy surge of blood. And, after such a long time, I remembered the thing Buntu and I had buried in me. I felt it as if it had just entered. I felt it again as it floated away on the surge. I would be ready for another month. Ready as always, each and every month, for new beginnings.

And Buntu?

I'll be with him, now. Always. Without our knowing, all the trying events had prepared for us new beginnings. Shall we not prevail?

19

PEGGY HOFFMAN

*Breathe, Scuttle*

There is a paper heart on the sidewalk
left by the bagwoman
in the middle of a storm.
She talks at night to the stars
when she finds them
or closes one eye to the blinking light
of the tavern sign.
In the dark, sometimes a boat slides across the ice
a cabbie honks his horn
and the cold breath of girls
spells words in the air.
The moon shines in a puddle
an oyster in oil, a pearl
the air is cold, the sky breathes
there is wonder in the world.
My mind hangs loosely, she says to the newsie,
like a tear on a stick.
Serenade me.

## Hallowe'en Eve

It could be the 5th of July
and ghosts would still web my skin.
I look out the window
and their faces, like etchings,
are frozen on the pane.
Their beards streak the sky
Their laughs are the electric hum in the air.
Bare branches breach to me
the skeleton of an embrace.

In this quiet lamp-lit room
I carve dates under photographs.
Completed histories
Epitaphs for the living.

BRIAN BARTLETT

*Love Poem During A Weather Report*

Today's high in Jerusalem: 30°.  And
I gaze, suddenly I gaze, leaning
closer to our TV — that fact
glowing like a wild crimson flower
picked and cradled by you, then
shipped back overseas, to me.  Montreal
falters into autumn, brown leaves
catching on our balcony rails.  Adrift
on our bed, adrift in these months that
hold you nations distant, I wander
into the word *J . e . r . u* . . . . Absence
fades in the valleys and orange groves.
Black smoke of practicing war-machines
blows in any direction but yours.  The gazelles
you mentioned in your last letter
dart between the *J* and the *m*.
In the desert, where the sun tightens
its fierce hold all day, you feel
so small, a bit of earth drowning in sand —
but wait, moment by moment I'm getting
closer, hiking empty-handed through
those four syllables; don't be startled
if waking one morning you feel me
holding you closer than heat . . . .

## All Corpses Are Equal

A tragicomedy by
Shie Min

Translated and adapted by
Henry Beissel
&
Jia-Lin Peng

CHARACTERS:  She, forty-six year old Ah Lan
He, a corpse, inflatable; forty-eight year old Fatty Jin

SET:  The stage is empty except for two stands (SR & SL), each with two wigs and several garments. Next to them a few props.

*SHE enters, pushing a cart, on which there is a body covered with a white sheet.*

SHE  *(covers her face with a white handkerchief and whines theatrically)* Oh, Fatty Jin, are you really dead? You died like a worm-bitten apple falling from a tree, like a balloon suddenly popped. Heaven is merciless. It allows me to burn you to ashes. *(stops, removes the handkerchief from her face and grins. Her facial expressions change quickly, grandly and comically. When she gets excited, she turns cross-eyed)* I should weep for him, but I can't help laughing when I think of what he said just a few days before he died. He came here making absurd demands. I thought he was joking. But now, he really lies dead on this cart. *(glances at her watch; to the corpse)* My friend, I'm afraid in fifteen minutes I'll burn you to ashes. So please say farewell to the world. *(slaps the body)* Don't spread your arms and legs like this! Even in death you put on airs. *(pushes his legs together, but as soon as she releases them they spread apart again. After two or three tries she gives up.)* Is he ever stubborn! *(to the audience)* Ladies and Gentlemen! This is our County Crematorium. I am the director of it, the make-up woman and — most of the time — the cremator as well. Before I was appointed to this post I worked in the County Hardware Cooperative. He, Fatty Jin, was the Party Secretary and the manager of the Cooperative. He considered me a trouble-maker because I liked to criticize the leadership. One day he said to me,

23

SHIE MIN

leadership entrusts you with an honorable job. You are transferred to the Crematory. There you will have to deal only with the dead. The dead never make mistakes, so you will get along fine with them. Nothing for you to criticize anymore."... And so, here I am. I've been here for two years already. It's a good job. Everyone must die, and all the dead are under my authority. That makes my position powerful and very important, don't you agree? ... Take Fatty Jin, for instance. Not long ago he bossed me around — but now it's my turn. *(laughs)* I must admit, as I speak of him I experience a strange mixture of emotions. — Move over a bit, Fatty. *(moves the body and sits next to it on the cart)* He and I grew up together. We entered the government service together. *(smiles ridiculously)* During the Cultural Revolution he was supposed to have been criticized by the revolutionary masses because he was a person in power. Instead, he organized the masses to criticize *me*, a powerless nobody. Once he punched me so violently on the nose that I turned cross-eyed. *(crosses her eyes)* Who wants to marry a woman with such ugly eyes? As a result I'm still a spinster. *(sighs, then laughs)* Oh, Fatty Jin, you shouldn't have died so early. I wanted to get even with you. There's something I've wanted to tell you. Do you want to listen? *(Suddenly jumps from the cart.) Yes!* Someone told me about a way to breathe new life into a dead man. Why don't I try it? Let's see...I have all the necessary equipment. *(Takes a bicycle pump out from beneath the cart.)* Here is my bicycle pump ... A valve. *(Takes out an air valve and inserts it in his shoe.)* Stick it in his foot. Now pump. *(pumps)* I'll fill his body with air. — This will bring you back to life, Fatty Jin, long enough so that I can ask — you — a — few — questions! *(pumping)* One-two, one-two!

*She pumps rhythmically; the corpse slowly rises rhythmically too until he sits on the cart with his legs dangling over the edge. She draws back from him. He is bald and dressed in grey Mao tunic and trousers, both of which are brand new. The rouged circles on his round cheeks give away a shoddy make-up job.*

SHE    There! You're as good as new.

HE    *(Slowly opens his eyes and rolls them cautiously. Opens his mouth, but there is no voice; shakes his head like a wet mop; after much effort he articulates:)* A! B! C! D! *(pause)* Mama, Papa, Brother, Sister, Chairman Mao, Chairman Mao ... *(sings)* do, ti, la, so, fa, mi, re, do! *(Giggles happily; she cannot help giggling too. With an exotic accent.)* Who ... are ... you?

24

SHE     *(to audience)* Beware, he has become a foreign devil! *(imitating his accent)* I ... am ... I!

HE     *(points to his nose)* Who ... am ... I?

SHE     You are Fatty Jin, *(changes her tone)* — our most honourable Party Secretary and the manager of the County Hardware Cooperative!

HE     *(blinks)* I am the Party Secretary — Secretary Jin? *(grins arrogantly)* Then I'm the number one man! But wait a minute! I'm not dead, am I?

SHE     Yes, you are!

HE     But that's impossible.

SHE     You died two days ago and you've been dead ever since. Yesterday, we had a grand memorial rally for you here.

HE     Are you sure? Who are you anyway? — Oh, I remember. You are Ah Lan ... I must be dreaming. But then I'm alive. *(Bites his finger to make sure he is alive.)*

SHE     Careful! If you puncture your skin, I can't keep you alive even for ten minutes!

HE     My head is spinning. First, you say I'm dead, now you say I'm alive. What am I — dead or alive?

SHE     *(giggles)* You have been resurrected. I've resurrected you by pumping your dead body full of air.

HE     *(suddenly loses his temper)* A likely story! How dare you lie to the leadership! A fool like you could never resurrect a dead man. Pumping air into a corpse — what nonsense! *(slaps his palm sharply against the cart)* You are a liar!

SHE     Just look at him! I have hardly finished pumping up his roly-poly corpse and already he's putting on airs! *(to him)* What I've told you is true! I've resurrected you with this *(shows him the pump)*. I attached a valve to your foot and pumped your body full of air till you started to breathe again!

25

HE    Is this really true? *(looks at his foot)* Yes, there is a valve. *(has a brainstorm; smiles)* Good, very good! *(jumps down from the cart)* Listen carefully and make a note of every word! *(Crossing his hands behind his back, he paces back and forth across the stage. She pretends to write.)* Most honoured comrade chairman: under your wise leadership, *we* have made an invention which will completely change the world, change the future of mankind, and guarantee the triumph of the revolution! I ... I... *(searching for words)*.

SHE   *(addresses audience)* What an opportunist! Disgusting, isn't he? But I have no time to listen to his twaddle! — I say, Fatty Jin! *(He doesn't answer. She switches to a reverent tone.)* Secretary Jin!

HE    *(with the affectation of modesty so typical of officials)* Yes. How are you? How is your work going? Nice to see you! So long! *(leaves)*

SHE   Hold on, Fatty Jin! I have a few questions to ask you. That's why I resurrected you.

HE    You? Resurrected me? *(reproachfully)* You're a born trouble-maker, aren't you! Even now that I'm dead you won't stop bothering me. *(impatiently)* Speak up, then! What is it you want to ask me?

SHE   *(pointing to her eyes)* Look at me! Do you see anything special?

HE    I see a face.

SHE   *(pointing to her eyes)* Look here!

HE    Your nose?

SHE   Don't play games with me! Look at these horrible eyes!

HE    Horrible? ... No! They're beautiful. So bright! Everyone knows your eyes can see through things.

SHE   Please! *(mildly)* Have you forgotten? At one of those struggle sessions during the Cultural Revolution, you struck my nose and made me cross-eyed. *(smiles)* But I have forgiven you.

26

HE     *(to audience)* She has forgiven me? *(grins briefly)* That's strange, considering it wasn't my fault. In those days everyone was crazy, remember. If I hadn't struggled against her, she would have struggled against me. *(to her)* So what if I struck you? What can I do about it now?

SHE     I want you to answer my questions.

HE     What for? I'm dead.

SHE     I know. But you still have to answer my questions.

HE     Good heavens! Haven't I done enough for you already? *(counts on his fingers)* I had your file revised. I saw that you were repaid all the money we'd taken from your salary. I rehabilitated you. And —

SHE     And you sent me to the crematory! ... It's not a question of work or money .... It's a question of truth.

HE     *(laughs)* Truth? What truth? The dead can't tell the difference between truth and falsehood.

SHE     I thought the opposite was true — that only the truth survives.

HE     You're naive, Ah Lan.

SHE     I must have the truth and you're going to tell me.

HE     Ever the trouble-maker, aren't you?

SHE     You never told the truth, have you? Now you must .... Why did you send me to the crematorium, why?

HE     *(as if he were in a struggle session)* All right, all right. I confess. I ... I ... *(moves his hand as if to wipe a stain from his imagination)* I wanted to ... eh ...

SHE     To what?

HE     *(timidly)* To wipe out ...

SHE     To wipe out what?

HE     I ... I wanted to wipe out the memory of ...

27

SHE    Of what?

HE    I couldn't bear to look in your eyes. Alright? *(grins)* The dead don't care how ugly your eyes are. *(pause)* To put you out of mind, I had to put you out of sight.

SHE    *(after a moment's silence)* These may be the first true words you've ever spoken. Well ... I suppose I can forget you.

HE    *(embarrassed)* Thank you, thank you so much! ... Good-bye! *(about to leave)*

SHE    Wait! I have another question!

HE    Another question?

SHE    Yes. And I want more of the same kind of truth.

HE    No, Ah Lan. Please, bring me back to death, deflate me, let me rest in peace — please!

SHE    Not until you've answered the question — truthfully.

HE    Have you no shame to trouble the dead? *(a brief pause)* Alright, alright. What do you want to know?

SHE    Fatty, tell me honestly... *(with passion)* When we were young did you really ... really ... love me?

HE    I? Love you? ... Huh! How could I have loved you?

SHE    What? You deny it? *(takes out a thick bundle of letters)* Look! What are these? They're love letters you wrote me twenty-five years ago.

HE    Twenty-five years ago? And you've kept them all this time? *(touched)* Ah Lan, you ... you are truly —

SHE    I've kept them because I wanted to burn them with you. Now you say you never loved me. Let the audience be the judge. I'll read them, every one of them, out loud, now, right here, to the audience.

HE    No, no, you can't do that! It's ... it's an invasion of privacy. *(amiably)* Ah Lan, I *did* love you. I truly loved you.

SHE    *(wipes away tears)* At last he has spoken from the bottom of his heart. But that's not enough. *(to him)* I want the audience to know exactly what you did *that* night. Let's reenact the scene for them, together.

HE    In every detail?

SHE    In every detail.

HE    That's going too far! *(looks at her)* ... Alright, alright. Let's. Seeing that I'm dead, what've I got to lose? Compared with what people do in movies nowadays, what we did was pretty tame anyway.

SHE    I was only twenty-two at the time.

HE    *(straightens his back)* And I was twenty-five. We were childhood friends. We'd played together. We'd gone to school together. Then we both worked for the government. She was a pretty and a hard-working girl, but she had one terrible flaw — a sharp tongue! She never hesitated to criticize the leadership. She wasn't afraid of anybody. So she upset many people in power. And yet, I loved her. I had to tell her I loved her. One evening, we sat side by side on two boulders by a brook.

SHE    *(sets two little stools side by side; to Jin)* You sit there. And I sit here. — It was I who began the conversation. I said, "Little Fatty" — we all called him "Little Fatty" in those days — "What's on your mind?" I asked.

HE    *(shy)* Nothing special ... *(scratching the sand with his foot; picks a stem of grass and bites it.)* And how about you? What's on your mind?

SHE    You're supposed to answer me. *I* asked the question.

HE    Yes, of course. *(pause)*

SHE    I know what's on your mind.

HE    You know?

29

SHIE MIN

SHE    Yes I do.

HE    I have something to tell you.

SHE    So, tell me.

HE    Ah Lan ... you ... you are ... a fine comrade ... We ... we ... have grown up together. I ... I ... I ...

SHE    Go on. Don't just "I ... I ... I ..."

HE    I can't. I just can't. My tongue is like a stone. I'm trembling ....

SHE    Are you sick?

HE    No. I'm alright. *(he clears his throat)* I want to tell you, Ah Lan, I ... I ... love you! *(Pause. They glance at each other from the corner of their eyes. As soon as their eyes meet, they turn their heads back.)*

SHE    Is it true? You really —

HE    I swear it's true.

SHE    And will you always love me?

HE    Always, always, always! Ah Lan, you are such a wonderful girl! — *(hugs her abruptly)*

SHE    *(pushes him away)* What are you doing, you old goat?

HE    You asked me to reenact what we did that night — in every detail!

SHE    Well, yes — that's enough. We needn't go any further. *(as if in a reverie, to herself)* Not that I'll ever forget that night! It was the happiest night of my life! *(recovers)* Fatty Jin, you must tell me! Why did you desert me after that? How could you have done such a heartless thing ... after you ... after we —

HE    Don't blame me! It wasn't my fault!

SHE    What do you mean, it wasn't your fault! Who deserted whom?

HE    *(angrily)* Yes, it was I who deserted you, but it was your fault. You have no one to blame but yourself.

30

SHE    Why? What did I do wrong? I loved you, I was loyal to you —

HE    You know very well what I'm talking about. It's your venomous tongue. You can't keep your mouth shut. That's your misfortune! Need I remind you what you called Magistrate Lin? ... A bureaucrat!

SHE    So what?

HE    A bureaucrat!

SHE    So what?

HE    You said it to his face!

SHE    It was true.

HE    True, true — don't pretend! You know I got into trouble over that. I never told you exactly what happened. Well, he summoned me to his office and said, "Comrade Little Jin, I have good news for you. I've recommended you for promotion to district head! But there's one condition. You must sever your relationship with Ah Lan."

SHE    He said that?

HE    Yes. And that's not all. He said, *(continues to mimic the magistrate)* "Ah Lan totally disregards the rules of the Party. She attacks the leadership! It is clear that she has no respect for the revolution. You must make a clean break with her. I give you a month from today. If you comply, we will announce your new appointment. Please understand that there's nothing personal in this. It is a test of your loyalty to the Party."

SHE    The Party?! So that's it. At last I understand! After twenty-five years I find out what really happened! Oh, Fatty Jin, Fatty Jin, you cast me aside for a promotion!

HE    *(angrily)* I obeyed the leadership. It would've been better for you if you'd obeyed the leadership too instead of forever criticizing them. And what's wrong with being promoted for the sake of the revolution? What greater honour is there? If you'd followed my example things would've gone differently for you. Not once in my life have I contradicted the leadership. *(Slaps his chest. There is a loud hissing as the air begins to leak from his body.)* I always do

31

what the leadership wants me to do, always think what they want
me to think! *(The hissing grows louder. He appears frightened.
He presses his belly. The hissing grows even louder.)* Damn!
*(with a weeping tone)* I'm leaking!

SHE      *(presses his belly)* Yes, you're leaking air.

HE      *(sits up on the cart)* I'm dying all over again. Ah Lan, I'll give
you a final piece of ... advice ... Watch your tongue! ... Never say
a word against the leadership! *(lies down slowly on the cart)*

SHE      *(pokes a finger at his belly)* He's leaking badly and we haven't
finished talking. ... Watch my tongue? Never say a word against
the leadership? ... Is it worth going on talking with him? *(Pause)*
Yes, I'll find out where he's leaking. *(examines him)* There's a
leak on his forehead ... And here's another. Oh well. It's a good
thing I have got some adhesive tape. *(Puts a piece of adhesive tape
on his forehead, another on his chin.)* Now, let's try once again.
*(pumping)* Arise, Fatty Jin. Arise! Up, up, up!

*He stirs rhythmically. Slowly he rises up.*

HE      *(Opens his eyes, pats his chest, opens his mouth, then tries to
sing.)* La-la-la-la, ya-ya-ya-ya!

SHE      Fill him with air and he starts singing!

HE      *(with an exotic accent)* Who ... am ... I?

SHE      He's forgotten again who he is ... You're Fatty Jin. I used to call
you Little Fatty.

HE      *(Leaps to his feet. Acting like an ancient official in the Peking
Opera, he strokes a long imaginary beard. Faces audience across
the cart. Suddenly slaps the palm of his hand against the cart.)*
You — you shameless woman — how dare you come before me
without kneeling?

SHE      Heavens, now he thinks he's a feudal lord! *(defiantly)* You're not
in the Peking Opera or the Ming Dynasty!

HE      *(very theatrical)* Bring me my sword! Off with your head!

SHE      Wake up, you bloated buffoon!

32

HE     *(changed)* Very well, we are revolutionary humanists. I'm prepared to give you a last chance. *(loudly)* Step forth, Red Guards! Put a paper hat on this reactionary devil's head and parade her through the streets!

SHE    Such a fashionable punishment!

HE     Damn you! *(touches the crown of his head)* Where is my cap? *(impatiently)* My cap, my cap!

SHE    Cap? What cap?

HE     The cap I brought all the way from Peking. The cap I left in your care — that you promised to keep for me.

SHE    Is that cap so important to you?

HE     Of course! Before I died, I came here to make a special request. I asked you to put the cap on my head before I was sent to the furnace. You promised! Now where is it? *(slaps the crown of his head)* Where is it?

SHE    What a funny man! *(laughing, teasingly)* What cap? I know nothing of any cap.

HE     You lie! ... And don't you laugh at me! Who do you think you are? *(suddenly changes his tone)* Oh, what a memory I have! Now I recognize you again. Comrade Ah Lan — how are you? How is your work at the crematory going? Naturally, you love it! Such an important position! To have authority over every dead man or woman in the province. *(pause)* In fact, I'll let you in on a secret. You wouldn't have got this job without the approval of the leadership. Now I can tell you — I'm the one who recommended you for this honorable and important job. I also used my influence to get you promoted quickly to head of the Crematory. Your rank now is twenty-third on the civil-servant ladder — on the same level as commune chairman. Aren't you grateful?

SHE    *(with irony)* Thank you for your patronage!

HE     And one good turn deserves another, right? — Ah Lan, a few days ago — was it the fifth? — I came here walking on a cane. Do you remember?

33

SHE     You forgot your cane. I've kept it for you. Here. *(She takes a cane from beside one stand and hands it to him.)*

HE      Thank you. I also carried a box.

SHE     That's right. You had it under your arm.

HE      I came limping into your office, out of breath. *(gasps breathlessly as he speaks)* How ... are you, Comrade Ah Lan?

SHE     I was alone in the office. You astonished me. *(They both reenact the scene naturally.)* Good heavens! Is that really you, old Jin?

HE      Yes. People say I'm not myself, but it's just that I'm ill.

SHE     You don't look well. What are you doing here in such a state?

HE      I've come to make a request. One good turn deserves another, remember. There's something you must do especially for me ... that is, when my corpse arrives here.

SHE     *(to audience)* He must be mad. No one comes to the crematory to book his own service ... Secretary Jin — that's a bad joke. You're a young man. You take a rest and you'll be alright. You'll see.

HE      *(sadly)* No, I'll never recover. I'm suffering from pulmonary emphysema, asthma, cancer of the stomach, angina pectoris and diabetes — to name just a few of my many ailments. The doctors tell me I've little time left. My days are numbered. I'm about to kick the bucket.

SHE     I'm so sorry to hear that ... especially considering the importance of buckets to the people's revolution.

HE      Help me! Let me enjoy a happy death!

SHE     If death makes you happy, who am I to spoil it for you. I'll do what I can.

HE      *(grows suddenly vigorous)* Thank you, thank you. You must help me, Comrade Ah Lan. After I've died, you must arrange a grand memorial gathering for me here. Even though I may not be a high cadre — my rank is eighteenth — there are very few people in the province with such a rank. Don't you agree I deserve some special consideration?

34

SHE     Absolutely. No problem. Don't worry. I'll do my best.

HE      Thank you, thank you so much. Ah Lan, you are such a good comrade ... I have only one last question to ask you. *(Pause)* Can the same furnace be used to cremate leading cadres as well as commoners?

SHE     Of course. No matter whose corpse it is — whether a cadre's or a peasant's — a corpse is a corpse. All corpses are equal.

HE      *(hollow laugh)* You're wrong, Ah Lan. Some corpses are more equal than others. For their contribution to the revolution, leading corpses should get special treatment.

SHE     You mean, corpses should be burned and buried according to rank? No, Comrade. You leading cadres have enough privileges in life as it is without perpetuating them beyond death. Our crematoriums may be the only real places of equality in the country because a furnace reduces every corpse equally to ashes. And that's the way it's going to stay.

HE      Ah Lan, the leadership has instructed you to cremate leading comrades in a special furnace. Why do you refuse to carry out your orders?

SHE     *(angrily)* I don't have to answer to you for it, or to anyone else. I simply refuse.

HE      How dare you! *(more mildly)* In Peking, there is a special crematory for leading cadres.

SHE     I don't care what they do in Peking. You can go to Peking and ask them to burn you there. But *here,* in this crematory, you will be burned like anybody else.

HE      *(smiles obsequiously)* Please, try to control your temper. *(Pause)* Alright, alright. Just use the ordinary furnace. I agree to be burned in the people's furnace ... as long as you promise to do me one favour. It's my final request. Ah Lan, *(pointing to the imaginary box in his hand)* in this box there is a cap. Please keep it for me. I want to be wearing it when my body is burned in the furnace. If you grant me this wish I will be eternally grateful — even in death. Will you?

35

SHE     Of course I will.

HE     You promise?

SHE     I promise. Besides, every man is free to choose what he wants to wear at the time of his cremation.

HE     *(smiles)* Then it's settled! Good. I entrust my cap to you. *(makes the action of handing the box)*

SHE     *(makes the action of accepting the box)* Alright, I promise.

HE     *(Seizes her hand. To audience)* You see, she *did* promise!

SHE     Damn! I've fallen into his trap.

HE     Say no more! Just give me the cap!

SHE     The cap?

HE     Yes, the cap?

SHE     Alright. *(She moves for the stand; he follows.)* Here you are.

HE     *(snatches the box)* My cap. My treasure! *(Sits on the cart; then opens the box and takes out the cap. It is a black gauze cap — the style which an official of the feudal era wears in the Peking Opera. He puts it on with an air of pomp, then starts to bob his head. The wings of the cap flap up and down.)* Very well — I'm ready, Ah Lan. It's time you cremate me. We can go now.

SHE     *(to audience)* Look at him. He clutches the black gauze cap for dear life — the coveted black gauze cap which is to symbolize his official position. Even in death he clings to the silly trappings of his rank and power. Hmm ... *(to him)* I cannot burn a living man.

HE     But I'm not living. I am a dead man. I only look alive — because I'm all puffed up. You did that. You pumped me up to make people think I'm alive. But it's all a lot of air. See? *(pinches himself)* Pull the plug and I'm gone. Dead. Forever ... Ppffft! ... *(sadly)* It's time you cremate me now. Do your duty. Or do you want me to walk to the furnace myself and jump in? *(starts to leave)*

36

SHE  *(seizes his arm)* Hold it! Don't you dare jump into the furnace with such a cap on your head!

HE  Why not? *(like a spoiled child)* I wanna wear it! I wanna wear it!

SHE  Tell me — what kind of society is this we live in?

HE  The new society, the socialist society. Why bother me with such a foolish question? Remember, I'm a party Secretary —

SHE  — who wears the cap of a feudal bureaucrat! Isn't it absurd? Who do you think I am?

HE  *(sardonically)* The director of the crematory, *(points his thumb up)* — top dog in this place.

SHE  Exactly. And I know what's right and what's wrong. I don't permit —

HE  *(cuts in fiercely)* How dare you refuse someone five ranks higher than you! You take orders from me, you understand? I could phone the leadership and have you dismissed on the spot.

SHE  If that would make you happy, go ahead. But no matter what you say or do, I'll burn you without that black gauze cap on your head. And there's nothing you can do about it.

HE  But you promised. One should keep one's promises.

SHE  When I promised, I never imagined what kind of cap you had in the box.

HE  Ah Lan, dear Ah Lan, don't be mean. Please, do it. Just for me. It won't harm anyone. It's just a black cap. What difference does it make to you? No one'll ever know.

SHE  I refuse.

HE  *(beats his breast)* You are being unreasonable, absolutely unreasonable! I've worked hard for thirty years. I've sacrificed my life in the service of the revolution! Now, all I ask is to be burned with a cap on my head. Am I to be denied such a little consideration? *(she giggles)* Be serious! Listen to me! *(switches tone)* You know, after I don't know how many generations, I'm the only one in my whole family ever to attain a position in government. Am I not entitled to bear this symbol of my achievement — to have my ancestors feel proud as they greet me in heaven? *(she bursts into laughter)* You've run the cremator long enough. What is so unusual about a man who wants to look good at his funeral? Properly attired according to his earthly achievements. Every old country hag wants to be buried in her Sunday best. Why should you refuse *me* my cap? *(she laughs)* Will you comply with my wish or not? *(she shakes her head, laughing)* ... How can you be so cruel! *(starts to sob)*

SHE     Good heavens! I've never seen a grown man cry like a baby! *(he wails even louder)* Don't cry, poor Little Fatty. Please don't cry.

HE      *(recovers composure immediately)* So you'll grant me my wish? *(points to the cap)*

SHE     Alright, alright, I'll burn you with the cap on your head ... on one condition!

HE      What condition? Tell me! I'll do anything you ask!

SHE     We shall enact another event from our early days for the audience.

HE      *(to audience)* I think her secret ambition is to become an actress. *(to Ah Lan)* Alright. If you insist — as long as I get my cap.

SHE     You will. Now we must reenact the event *exactly* as it happened. Agreed?

HE      *(Grins obscenely; bobs his head making the wings on his cap flap up and down.)* Agreed. No reason for me to be shy if you're not.

SHE     *(to both him and audience)* It happened long ago — one day in the early fifties, when we were young lovers. That very morning you'd been promoted to Vice District Magistrate. Later that afternoon you and I visited your grandmother.

HE      *(lively)* Right. We visited granny. After all her years of devotion to me — raising me from the age of three — I wanted to tell her the news of my promotion.

SHE     So, you play yourself. I'll play your grandmother.

HE      *You!* — my granny! *(laughs)* ... Sure, why not ... I mean it's only a play.

38

SHE     First, we must dress up for our parts.

*He takes off the cap and removes his tunic. She gives him a wig, then places another on her own head. She puts on an old-fashioned dress that is hanging on a stand. She picks up the cane. At once, he becomes a young man, and she a slouching grey-haired old lady. He exits.*

HE      *(reenters)* Granny! Granny!

SHE     *(gasps and pounds his back)* Ah-h — Little Fatty!

HE      *(excitedly)* How are you, Granny? I've got good news!

SHE     *(Though she is pleased to see her grandson, she pretends to be angry.)* You heartless monkey, you haven't come to visit me for ages!

HE      Don't be angry, Granny. I'm so busy these days. I've missed you night and day. The moment I could get away, I ran to see you.

SHE     You haven't lost your glib tongue, you handsome monkey. Alright, tell me. What's the good news?

HE      *(like a little boy)* Granny, you're looking at the new Vice District magistrate. My appointment was announced this morning.

SHE     *(smiles, wipes away happy tears)* Thank heaven: finally you are an official. For so many generations we've had only farmers, barbers, servants, maids, farmhands, butchers, sedan-chair-carriers and rickshaw pullers in the family, but never an official. You're the first one! At last, we can stand up proud among the masters of the country. And we owe it all to the Communist Party, to Chairman Mao. I'll be sure to burn joss sticks before his portrait this evening .... By the way, are you hungry? You and Ah Lan must stay for dinner. We must celebrate! I'll kill a chicken.

HE      Please, Granny, calm down. I'm only Vice District Magistrate.

SHE     Only?

HE      The position is not *that* important.

SHE     Not *that* important? Of course it's important! It means you'll have millions of people under your command. I'm so happy for you. Who would've thought when your parents died and left you to me. How much I sacrificed and suffered to raise you! And it's all borne fruit. You've become an important person! I can close my eyes now and die without regret.

HE     Don't talk about death, Granny. The good life is just beginning.

SHE     We must all die. I'm a sick old woman. I know that soon I'll leave this world. Little Fatty, there's one thing you must do for me when I die.

HE     I'll do anything, Granny. But please, don't talk about dying.

SHE     *(pulls him close to her)* Little Fatty, many years ago I worked as a maid for the family of an official. When the official's mother died, there were special graveclothes made for her —

HE     *(quickly)* Don't worry, Granny. When you pass away, I'll be sure to buy brand new clothes for you.

SHE     What I'm talking about are *special* graveclothes.

HE     *Special* graveclothes? What do you mean? Everybody is supposed to be buried in the same standard clothes. That's what we had a revolution for.

SHE     Silly boy! The graveclothes I'm talking about are something quite particular.

HE     Quite particular? What's particular about graveclothes? People are buried in ordinary clothes.

SHE     Of course, ordinary people. But it's different with officials. They have graveclothes according to their rank.

HE     All that's a matter of the past.

SHE     What d'you mean: it's a matter of the past? You're an official now, are you not? You've just become an official. We are no longer ordinary people. Your rank may not be very high and I may not be entitled to wear a robe with beautiful pictures like dragons, phoenixes, the sun, the moon or with peonies, but I do deserve something more than a commoner. I want to be buried wearing a

40

robe with a big golden character for "good fortune" embroidered upon it. I've suffered all my life, it's true. But my grandson has at last become an official. So, in fact, I do have good fortune. Will you grant your old granny this last wish?

HE     *(scratches his head)* I ... *(knits his eyebrows)* I ... *(grins)* I'll do anything for you, Granny — but where could I possibly find such a museum piece?

SHE     At a stage costume factory. A man from our village will go to Peking next month. I'll ask him to buy it for me.

HE     But I ... *(turns his pocket inside out)* I don't have any money.

SHE     *(reproachfully)* I don't need your money. I've been saving for a long time.

HE     Alright, Granny, it's not a question of money. We communists aren't feudal lords, we're servants of the people. It'd be wrong to do such a thing.

SHE     Are you ... I don't believe this ... Are you refusing your old Granny her dying wish? After all the years of suffering I endured for your sake, the sacrifices I made to bring you up to become an official? I was like a mother to you.

HE     Oh I know, dear granny, I do love you. But I have to refuse on principle.

SHE     On principle? What does that mean? On principle. Don't give me any of your fancy words. Just tell me plainly, will you or won't you?

HE     I won't. I can't.

SHE     *(strikes the floor with the cane)* How dare you! You may be District Magistrate outside my house —

HE     — Vice District Magistrate —

SHE     — well, here you're my grandson. I can still give you a thrashing. Bend over! *(he, giggling, bends over)* I'll show you. *(raises the stick high, but beats lightly)* That'll teach you to defy me! *(He wails in a theatrical voice. She stops thrashing him and starts to weep.)* Heavens above, what terrible sins have I committed in my

41

previous life!  Is this my punishment — to have raised such a faithless, ungrateful grandson?  I nurtured you like my own child —

HE    Don't cry, Granny! *(gently pats her back)* Please, don't cry! It's not good for your health.  Will you listen to me, Granny?  I have something to ask you.

SHE    I'm listening.

HE    Do you love the new society?

SHE    Yes, of course.  But what does the new society have to do with the kind of clothes I wish to be buried in?

HE    Everything!  That's just it, Granny.  Everything.

SHE    What do you mean?  Why should Chairman Mao bother about the clothes I want to wear for my funeral?

HE    You don't understand.  There was a time when aristocratic families claimed aristocratic graveclothes as their right.  That was the ancient custom.  Everybody lived and died according to his social class and rank.  But if all of us continue to act according to ancient customs, the new society will no longer be new but the old one all over again. *(She turns her face away.  He bends over.)* Alright. Go on then.  Keep thrashing me if you're still angry.  But remember — *(She strikes a brutal blow on his buttocks.)* Ouw-w! Granny never beat me so cruelly!

SHE    Hah!  The play is finished. *(Throws away the cane.  Takes off her wig.)* Now, tell me the truth:  did granny finally insist on getting her *special* graveclothes?

HE    Of course not! ... Now that's enough of play-acting.  I've satisfied the terms of our agreement.  You must keep your promise. *(Picks up the cap, puts it on his head.)* Now, let out the air and take me to the furnace!

SHE    You still insist on wearing that cap?

HE    You promised.

SHE    After all you said to your grandmother?

HE     A promise is a promise.

SHE    Even an uneducated old woman like her understood that there can be no privileges in the new society.

HE     My case is totally different. The circumstances are different. My position is different. Times have changed.

SHE    You can say what you like, my answer remains the same: I'm not going to cremate you in that cap.

HE     And you can say what you like, my orders remain the same: I deserve to wear it and you're going to cremate me in it! I've never met such an obstinate, incorrigible person as you. I warn you. I've got a lot of influence. I can still get you into deep trouble.

SHE    You have as much influence as a bag of hot air. Have you forgotten that you're dead already? Besides, you should know I'm not the kind of woman who yields to threats.

HE     *(a new tack)* Don't upset yourself, Ah Lan. I was only joking. Oh, my darling, I have a confession to make on my death cart. I look into your eyes and I know that I am guilty. I betrayed you. I struck you. I had you sent to the crematory .... But believe me my heart has bled for every time I hurt you. My life has been miserable. It's true I married another woman, but I never loved her. I never had a happy hour with her.

SHE    You're raving.

HE     That's why I died so young. Ah Lan, I never loved anyone but you. I should've married you. Then all this *(indicates his condition and the surroundings)* would never have happened.

SHE    *(more or less touched)* The past is past. There's no use dwelling on what might have been.

HE     Ah Lan, tell me: do you remember the stories of women who were buried alive with their men?

SHE    That was thousands of years ago. In ancient times, when a slave-owner died, his woman might be buried alive with him. Why do you ask?

43

HE    Some women positively wanted to be buried alive with their lovers. Remember? Once we saw an opera about a girl who jumps into her lover's tomb. Then they turn into a couple of butterflies. These were women of the noblest kind — like you, Ah Lan! Oh, my beloved Ah Lan, let's go to the furnace together! Such a supreme act of love would beget a legend. We'll be an inspiration to poets! Immortal! Let's burn in the furnace together and be reborn again from our ashes like two butterflies. That's how we'll live forever — happily in love!

SHE   You've gone stark raving mad! I'm not happily in love with you. I couldn't love a man like you if I wanted to. And as for jumping in a furnace with you —

HE    *(rolls up his sleeves)* Never mind! No matter! Love me or love me not, you'll go to the furnace with me. The lovers in flames! Or do you think I'm such a fool that I'd let you run off with my black gauze cap? *(Approaches her; she shrinks away.)* I deserved a black gauze cap in life; I'll wear a black gauze cap in death!

      *Music. A farcical chase begins. She eludes him nimbly and makes faces at him; he is enraged. Finally, he stumbles and falls to the floor; she runs up to him and wrenches the valve from his foot.*

SHE   Time to die, Fatty Jin.

      *With the sharp sound of hissing he springs up onto the cart and lies down, the air quickly leaking out of him.*

HE    *(Clutches the cap with both hands.)* Don't touch my black gauze cap! Don't take it off! Don't ... don't ... please ... *(deflated)*

SHE   *(Lifts his hands away from his head and drops them to his sides. Seizes the cap from his head and throws it as far away as possible.)* To hell with you and your cap, Fatty Jin. *(covers him with the sheet)* Men! Dead or alive, they're windbags! *(looks at her watch)* Time for cremation! *(Pushes the cart to the exit. Cut lights quickly.)*

### THE END

## The Guerilla Is Like A Poet

The guerilla is like a poet
Keen to the rustle of leaves
The break of twigs
The ripples of the river
The smell of fire
And the ashes of departure.

The guerilla is like a poet.
He has merged with the trees
The bushes and the rocks
Ambiguous but precise
Well-versed on the law of motion
And master of myriad images.

The guerilla is like a poet.
Enrhymed with nature
The subtle rhythm of the greenery
The inner silence, the outer innocence
The steel tensile in-grace
That ensnares the enemy.

The guerilla is like a poet.
He moves with the green brown multitude
In bush burning with red flowers
That crown and hearten all
Swarming the terrain as a flood
Marching at last against the stronghold.

An endless movement of strength
Behold the protracted theme:
The people's epic, the people's war.

1968

EDGAR MARANAN

## Foliage And Tiger Fire

The forest looms as footnote to this war and history.
A firefight is a burst in time, rivals strafing dreams.
Rattle thus of arguments, war spews a logic of conquest:
Rations and logistics expedite the murder of a populace.

Rustling, the leaves conceal the silent pores
As if the wind brings nothing but cool treesong
For the wedge of invading men in combat green
Girding for a war ten thousand miles from home.
On wing: but the birds do not disperse in fear
As if the tiger were always part of the foliage
Not threatening the forest hush, keeping tense
Like the limbs of raintrees about to be sprung.
Monsoons and time of soft earth stirring
Underfoot, when armies chew up the paddyfields
Where lean buffalo and cracked vehicles contend
For the sustenance of mud and cover of reeds.
Then the wind, rising from the outer sea of fear
Brings in the familiar banshee scream of steel
Contrails snaking in as though a dance of death
Unleash from racks a showerwhine of cluster hate
Upon ricestalks and the bastion of bamboo clumps.
Like straws the trees are mowed down by the blast
And a fireball, momentarily, blooms into a canopy
As battle eyes anticipate a burning swarm of men.
Yet the furtive enemy lives beneath pith helmets
Black clothes and rubber sandals keep their pace
Even as a mother with child is unfurled in flames.
It is but a day in twenty years of people's war.

Rustling, the leaves conceal the silent pores
As treesongs end with the anthem of tiger fire.
As the aliens flee with their gunships and camps
Victory staggers out of craters and a million tombs.

## *Los Baños Interlude I*

Perhaps tonight, then nothing more.
The months move about,
slinging their fists in the air,
the gradual chill that stirs the leaves
out of their stupor, a sleep that lasts
a thousand years.

She sits by the window, looks out
and exclaims: "the world always turns gray
at this time of day. . . .
and to have once thought that only
our words could save us."

## *Los Baños Interlude II*

The rain, like the beer in the run-down
sari-sari store, is warm. School children,
siblings of a lost generation, trace their way
home through the mud-filled roads.

Her name is Juana, *ang babaeng pinaglihi sa kangaroo*,
and they're off to see her at the carnival,
one peso per head. On the side, you can win
a can of pork and beans in a game of *beto-beto*.

Is this all there is to say about a town
famous for *buko* pie and *espasol*, and the hot springs
languishing with the dust of transients and tourists,
the memories of old people afflicted with rheumatism
and nostalgia?

Ah, but there is still Maria Makiling, whose breasts
are gathered up by the fog, pregnant by the warm
rain and the blood of rebels who never came down.

SERVANDO MACBANUA

## *Eastward The Winds Of Song*

For all their contours the hills
    look flat and low
as dewdrenched we nightwalk
    out of the primeval forest.
Our guns glint a dusky gray
    in the moonlight;
instinctively we merge with new-
    found shadows.
Farther, brown paddies form a
    maze of linear patterns
and sugar cane fields stretch
    as far as the eyes can see —
how alien at first the lowlands
    of our dreams!

      (Fleetingly with yet a longing
      we cannot name we look back
      at towering Taganhin majestic above
      the rugged mountain districts
      and smile. . . .)

From afar floats a morning
    lullaby — there!
In clusters of bamboo trees
    tacked on the silvery slopes
In wombs of creeksides
    mysterious and dark
stabs of light undulate from
    sparse and unfamiliar huts
beckoning the Red nomads of night.

*"Pasa bilis!"* our squad leader
    motions.
We hurry on with winged feet
    our hearts throbbing wildly
as eastward the winds of song
    draw us nearer, nearer,
to the land of the *haciendas*. . . .

November 1980

## Vulture Suya

Fadimatu Aliyu did not want to make vulture suya; she wanted to pack out of her father's compound and go to the College of Education in Kano.

The trouble began one day after her father had taken his midday meal and had called her to come take his plates. He was sitting under the flame tree, cleaning his teeth with a chewing stick.

It was near the end of the dry season, and the smell of the first rains, still far to the south, was a torment to Fadimatu. Gaunt, slow-moving cows grazed on the woven grass walls her brother Ahmadu had put up for shade and privacy. Their two remaining chickens — dull, yellow things — pecked at bits of paper by the highway. Cats with patches of fur missing from their tails and flies clinging to their sores had killed and eaten the young chicks.

Even if the rains came early, Nigerians would continue to suffer. Oil prices had dropped again. The traders had begun to hoard rice and oil and laundry soap.

But Fadimatu's father was growing rich. He took yards of the new and expensive European polyester satin to his tailor. He had several gowns made from this shimmering, clingy material. And fat! Two years ago Fadimatu had served him only one piece of meat in his stew; sometimes, to stop his complaining, she had cut it in three small pieces. In those days he cleaned the plate with his finger. Now she served him four, even five pieces of meat. His shiny gowns were stretched tight across his stomach. He was profiting from Nigeria's poverty. He was a bicycle repairman, and now that men could no longer afford the petrol and the repairs for their Peugot 504's, they were riding bicycles.

His son Ahmadu looked out for used bicycles and offered the owners a good price.

"Rice and oil and soap are essential commodities, yes," Malam Aliyu said. "But so is transportation." He cleaned and polished the bicycles; he fitted them with plaid seatcovers and red pedals from Taiwan, and he resold them at a great profit.

In one way, Fadimatu started the vulture suya trouble herself. When she came that day to the flame tree, her father began to reflect on his good fortune. He waved his chewing stick around in the air as he talked, and Fadimatu saw several vultures circling over the highway; likely, there had been another accident.

"There is no limit to what I can do," her father was saying. "I have *wayo*," he said, tapping his head with his forefinger to make the sign of European intelligence. "Because of this *wayo* there is nothing I care to waste. Even poverty has usefulness. *Kai*, even these ugly birds could have usefulness." He pointed with his chewing stick at the vultures overhead. Fadimatu wondered again about the accident. She turned to leave with the

49

plates, on which her father had left several fingerfuls of stew. But he motioned her to stay.

"Are these vultures not fowl, together with hens?" he asked. "And when they die, do they not lie wasted on the soil until they themselves are eaten by the living? And if they taste sweet to other vultures and to crawling things, would they not taste sweeter to a human being?"

Her father loved to think and he loved even more to talk.

"But father, look what they eat," Fadimatu said. "Their meat would not be sweet to us. It would be contaminated."

"Contaminated?"

"If Allah had meant for man to roast the flesh of vultures, then we would have vulture suya," Fadimatu said.

"Vulture suya," Malam Aliyu repeated. "Yes! Vulture suya!"

*"Haba!"* Fadimatu cried, covering her mouth with her hand. But it was too late.

Malam Aliyu called his son Ahmadu and told him to go into the bush and kill a vulture.

"But the vultures they are more beside the road," Ahmadu said. "Because they like accidents," he added.

"Then go to the road."

"Am I to use this?" Ahmadu took out the slingshot he had made from a strip of bicycle innertube.

"Why not?"

Ahmadu ran off, whistling. Malam Aliyu continued to walk up and down by the flame tree.

"Fadimatu? Why are you standing there?" he said. "Take my plates to the kitchen. And boil water. We will first taste the boiled flesh. If it is sweet, Ahmadu will dig a suya pit for roasting."

Before Fadimatu had even finished washing the plates, Ahmadu brought her a fat and fluffy young vulture. He watched while she killed it, plucked it, broke it into parts and dropped them in the boiling water.

"But I will not do this again," she whispered. "*Kai!* This idea is very bad! This vulture suya can only bring trouble to our family compound. What good can come of boiling and roasting the flesh of vultures?"

After a short time her father came into the kitchen.

"If the meat is sweet, I will mix a very good spice," he said. "Taste it now, Ahmadu."

The boy took a leg. He tore off a piece of meat with his teeth and ate it quickly.

"Very sweet," he said. He wiped the grease from his mouth.

That evening, when the sun was not so hot, Malam Aliyu and his son dug a suya pit under the flame tree. Malam Aliyu mixed a special blend of ginger and garlic and Maggie Cubes, and the following evening, offered pieces of roast vulture to visitors and people passing by.

50

A blind old man stopped to greet Malam Aliyu on his way home from the mosque. Malam Aliyu pushed Ahmadu towards the roasting skewers, that he might take one to the old man.

"*Kai!* This your chicken suya, it is too sweet," said the blind man.

A schoolmate of Ahmadu's jumped down from the mud wall. "No be chicken, *Baba*," he said, addressing the old man.

"Then what?" asked a relative of Malam Aliyu's, who had come by to ask for a small amount of money to buy laundry detergent.

The schoolboy accepted another stick of the skewered meat. He gnawed at a piece of gristle.

"Dog," he said.

"Dog?" The boy who was begging money turned to his uncle and his cousins. "No be dog," he said. "Maybe bush meat. Bush rat, maybe bush cat ... *sai Allah.*"

"Yes: only God knows," Malam Aliyu said. He quickly made up his own proverb. "Can man know the mother of every chicken?" he asked.


Every morning Ahmadu went off with his slingshot. He returned before the midday meal with a vulture for Fadimatu. She cut off its head and plucked it and pulled the meat off its bones. She cut the flesh into strips, pounded them with a flat stone, cut them and skewered them with onions on short, sharpened sticks.

Malam Aliyu sat by his suya pit under the flame tree.

"I will rest even as I am working," he said. Every evening at dusk he brought his cassette player out from his bicycle repair shop. He put on Dolly Parton or Don Williams or traditional Arab music and he encouraged men and boys to sit and talk, even if they had no money for suya.

Naturally he could sell his vulture suya for a very low price, and because his suya pit was on the main highway, many travellers stopped to rest and feed themselves. And because there was also a mosque next door, taxi and bus drivers began to pull in at Malam Aliyu's for the two evening prayers.

Soon the three other suya sellers were grumbling.

"What kind of chicken is this that Aliyu can sell it so cheaply?" said the first.

"Does he have magic to make one hen born some unnatural number of chicks?" said the second.

"Even his spices," said the third, who, it must be said, was stingy in his use of Maggie Cubes, "is it not too strange that this son of a bicycle repairman can learn well well the secret of suya spices?"

They met at each other's suya pits and stood looking past the cow and chicken suya sticks into the spitting flames.

"It is dogmeat," said one.

51

*"Haba!"* cried another. "How can it be dog when the meat is pale and not red? This meat is from a winged creature. Except they be flying dogs ...."

Finally one man sent his youngest daughter to spy on Fadimatu in her kitchen. The small girl saw Fadimatu plucking a large dark bird. She ran back to her father's compound.

"She is with one *Ungulu*," she told her father.

"A vulture? *Gaskiya?* You must tell me the truth."

"Allah!" the girl cried. "Big like this. So dark. And with the reddish head."

The suya sellers decided to send for Yakubu Mohammed, the local Inspector of Health. When he arrived they begged him to stop their competitor in any way he could.

"If you ask him for bribe, we will say nothing," said the first suya seller.

"If you demand his daughter, we will not know it," said the second suya seller.

"If you take from this son of a bicycle repairman his last kobo and demand his daughter and then drag him off to prison, we will say nothing," said the third suya seller. "But we beg you," he said, pounding his fist into the palm of his other hand, "We beg you to use any and all means to stop his vulture suya *disting*, because it is ruining us. Allah!"

Yakubu was happy to raid Malam Aliyu's compound. He looked forward to extra money, but he was even more interested in the bicycle repairman's daughter. Her refusal to friend the principal of her former school had made her famous. So stubborn was she that the principal had been forced to expel her. Even to think about this Fadimatu made Yakubu's manhood grow hard.

He begged his friend the Police Commissioner to lend him his new Peugot 505. He brought his most costly outfit to his junior brother and stood over the boy as he ironed it.

"Those coals are too hot for pressing a *baban riga*."

"They are not hot. Allah, you are disturbing," said the boy. He lifted the pale pink embroidered gown over his uncle's head and began to press the narrow-legged trousers. When Yakubu was dressed, he shook plenty of *One Man Show* cologne on his hair and *baban riga*, lifting the gown and pulling out the top of his trousers for a final splash of scent over his manhood.

He found Malam Aliyu sitting under the flame tree by his suya pit. Fadimatu had heard the 505, and she stood on the cool sand by the *zanamat* wall, watching the two men; her father, small and fat, ridiculous in his shiny green gown, and Yakubu Mohammed, the tall and very black young Health Inspector. He was driving the Police Commissioner's 505 — he himself had only a Raleigh bicycle. But he knew how to French kiss. This was what Fadimatu's friend Baby claimed.

"Not these our quick quick African kisses," Baby had added. "No: so slow, even as the Europeans kiss. *Kai*, they know how to enjoy! And if I tell you what he knows how to do with his hands! *Kai!* He knows us as we know ourselves!"

Fadimatu forced herself to listen to Yakubu and her father.

"Malam, let us come to the point," Yakubu was saying. "I must ask from you five hundred Naira in tax for this your vulture *disting*."

But her father refused.

"I will not dash you one kobo," he said. "I am an honest bicycle repairman and more recently suya seller; the giving or taking of bribe is a horror to me."

"But this your vulture suya is illegal," Yakubu said. "Nevertheless, bring four hundred naira and I will manage the thing."

"*Haba*," Malam Aliyu said.

"Okay. Bring one hundred naira," Yakubu said. "Or you will have yourself to blame. When you go to prison," he added.

"Prison?" Malam Aliyu laughed. "But my good friend Garba Mohammed is the Inspector of Prisons. It would be my pleasure to meet with him and discuss the state of Nigeria."

Yakubu stood. "You will have yourself to blame, Malam," he said. Fadimatu watched him begin to walk toward the main road. She saw him turn back when her father had lain down again on his mat. When she was sure he was walking towards her, she ran into the kitchen. There in the hot darkness, she retied her wrapper, licked her fingers to smooth her hair, and picked up the stunned vulture.

Yakubu stopped at the entrance to the cooking area. When Fadimatu came out of the kitchen with a large vulture, he entered and went straight to her.

"What is your intention with this evil bird?" he asked. He put his hands around the vulture.

Fadimatu looked down. Yakubu's hands were long, blue-black, and very sensitive looking.

"I will pluck it," she said.

"Ah." The bird was fluttering slightly in their arms.

"Please, you are disturbing me," Fadimatu said. Yakubu stepped back. Fadimatu put the vulture on a wood block and chopped off its head. She held it over a bowl to collect the blood.

After a moment Yakubu drew close again. "This is an offense," he said.

Fadimatu shrugged. "Tell that to my father," she said.

"And what of me? Do you not know who I am?" Yakubu asked.

"Of course I know you," she said. "You are one Yakubu Mohammed, Health Inspector for Jima Local Government. You are going up and down with your bicycle; you have been coming to my father with punctures, but today you have come with some big man's Peugot 505. It

53

resembles that of the Police Commissioner. Hold the bird, please." She took a pot from the fire and began to pour scalding water over the vulture.

When she pulled at a few feathers to test if they were loosened enough to be plucked, Yakubu grabbed one.

"Which is softer," he asked angrily, "this feather, or your arm?"

"If that is your only riddle, you will live long, Yakubu Mohammed, long and free from worry," Fadimatu answered.

"You know that I could put your father in prison for selling vulture suya," Yakubu said.

"Is this what you have come to tell me?"

"No." Yakubu pulled her to him. His erection was against the wet bird.

"Ah. You wish to friend me."

"Yes."

"But I do not wish to friend you," she said. "So we have nothing to discuss."

"Then you do not mind to see your father suffer in jail?"

Fadimatu laughed. "If my father goes to jail," she said, "he will be well fed — and I will be free."


The Health Inspector spent that afternoon at the Cool Spot Internation Hotel, drinking stout with the Police Commissioner, the bank manager, and the Inspector of English. From these men, and from the two schoolgirls who sat swinging their legs and drinking Fantas, he learned that Fadimatu's dream was to go to the College of Education in Kano.

"But what is this to me?" asked his friend the Police Commissioner. "Do not bother me again for my Peugot 505, I do not wish to help you friend the daughter of this bicycle repairman."

Yakubu also learned that Malam Aliyu's friend, the former Chief Inspector of Prisons, had died the year before, from fever. Yakubu waited for a few days to pass, and then returned to the Aliyu compound, this time in his ordinary clothes and riding his bicycle. When he arrived, Aliyu was standing at his suya pit, driving the suya sticks into the sand around the fire. After the evening greetings, Yakubu stood a moment, watching.

"I am just now hearing of your good friend's death," he said.

"You say?"

"Why, your good friend Garba Mohammed, the Chief Inspector of Prisons. Such a pity he died from fever."

Malam Aliyu went on driving the suya sticks into the sand.

"I suppose you expect me to think you are close friends with the new Chief Inspector of Prisons?"

Malam Aliyu turned.

"What do you want, Yakubu?" He reached in his pocket and took out a tight roll of Naira.

"Six hundred Naira."

"*Na wa o:* this is war!" Malam Aliyu cried. "My money will never reach six hundred Naira!"

"Then your daughter," Yakubu said quietly.

Malam Aliyu stared at him. "She is preparing my evening meal," he said.

Yakubu went to the entrance to the cooking area.

"*Salama alaikum,*" he called in greeting.

"*Alaikum salama,*" Fadimatu called back. "*Wannene?*"

"It's me, Yakubu Mohammed, the Health Inspector."

Fadimatu came out rubbing her eyes.

"My eyes are stinging from the smoke," she said.

Yakubu nodded, and they exchanged greetings. "If you don't friend me," he said abruptly, "I can prevent you from entering the College of Education in Kano."

Fadimatu frowned.

"How can you think I would friend you for such a small thing?"

Yakubu smiled. "This is in fact true," he said. "You refused your principal at Jimatown College."

Fadimatu shrugged.

"To me, it was not difficult."

Yakubu thought a moment. "Then friend me because I will bring you beautiful cloth," he said. "Fine indigo from Kano. Beautiful wax prints from Kaduna. Shoes from *Ingila*. Original. Blue jeans from *Amirka*."

"No," Fadimatu said. But between quick glances at his face, she was looking at his hands. She had been having fantasies about these hands. The two stood quietly, and as they stood, the sun dropped down behind the fields, and the night creatures began to hiss and spit and twitter.

"Fadimatu," Yakubu said quietly. "Friend me and I will use my manhood to sex you."

Fadimatu did not answer immediately, because she felt choked by the force of her heartbeat. When she did speak, her voice was also low and quiet.

"But do you imagine I am with that small button? Can I know pleasure?" And she added, teasing, "Am I not a good Muslim girl?"

Yakubu drew back.

"How will I answer this riddle?" he asked. His voice was gentle.

"You will have to search me," Fadimatu said. She pulled him into the zinc kitchen, and standing with one foot on a stool, drew his hand through the parting of her cloth wrapper.

And Yakubu became certain he had solved the riddle, because Fadimatu began to move her body and make sounds in her throat.

"My search tells me that for a Muslim girl you are one modern somebody," Yakubu said in her ear. "But definitely you are an obedient Muslim girl to save your father."

Fadimatu opened her eyes.

"Save my father?"

"Oh. Well. That is to say ... but since you didn't know your father offered you to me ... let's forget it now ... let's forget the whole matter." But Fadimatu had straightened, and she wouldn't let him put his hand back.

"My father?" she said. "My father? And what of my own intentions. Ha. See my body," she said, stepping out of the kitchen into the harsh light. "I will cover my body from you," she said, and she pulled her wrapper tightly around her hips. "What do you know of my body? Nothing. *Kai!* My father. Goats." She made a short hissing sound, and then walked out of the kitchen area, leaving Yakubu with his arms by his sides.

She spent the rest of the afternoon standing by the highway looking up, watching for vultures, shooting at them with a slingshot she had taken from a small boy on the path. As each vulture fell, stunned, she ran to it and carried it to a place on the road where an oncoming vehicle would be sure to hit it. In one instance a freshly stunned vulture was smashed against the windshield of an oncoming Peugot even before it hit the ground.

The next morning, when her father rose after the first call to prayer, he found a pile of vultures outside his hut. He turned one over with his foot. Its neck was broken, its head pushed into its wing. Another's legs were broken and dangling and its body was flattened and stiff with blood.

Malam Aliyu told Ahmadu to carry the vultures out to the bush. Then he followed Fadimatu around as she swept and did her morning work in the kitchen. He picked up a spoon and put it down again. He sniffed at a bag of grain and pushed a bundle of firewood with his toe. He stood over Fadimatu while she chopped onions into a large stew pot.

"This is very bad magic," he said.

"Then why not stop this your vulture suya *disting*?" Fadimatu said.

"*Disting* you are referring to is making me a rich somebody," he said.

Fadimatu shrugged, and went on chopping onions. When she had added five onions her eyes were full of tears. She threw down the knife and turned to her father.

"Why did you offer me to the Health Inspector?" she asked.

"Because I knew you had the strength to refuse him," her father said. "You are my daughter, aren't you?"

Fadimatu did not nod or smile.

"It was a trick! Fadimatu! You know that! If you were a boy, your intelligence would reach my own!"

56

But Fadimatu would not answer him. From that moment on she would not speak to him. He was forced to make up stories for visitors.

"My daughter cannot speak because of sadness. We are reaching the time when she must leave her father. She is sad to pack out of his compound to the College of Education in Kano." And Malam Aliyu reached into the front pocket of his new polyester gown and took out a small amount of money. He gave it to Fadimatu in front of the visitors. His son Ahmadu was jealous. The next time Ahmadu sold a bicycle, he kept part of the money. Months later Malam Aliyu found out, but by then he was losing his eyesight and was more afraid of being abandoned than of being cheated.

When Fadimatu did pack out of her father's compound, she had only the money he had given her, which would pay her school fees for one term, and another small sum she had saved from hawking cola nuts and coconut slices outside his bicycle shop. It was not enough to pay the fare for public transport. She was standing at the side of the road begging a lift when Yakubu Mohammed drove by. He hardly looked at her as he offered to take her to the city of Kano.

"In this your friend the Commissioner's 505?" Fadimatu laughed and climbed in.

"Let us pretend this is your own automobile," she said. "And let us pretend we are lovers." And so they drove to Kano, and Fadimatu did imitations of her father waving his chewing stick in the air, bragging about his special suya spice. By the time they reached Kano, Yakubo was smiling and laughing, and when Fadimatu got out of the car at the College gates, she blew him a kiss and promised to write.

57

MARTIN MOONEY

*Channels*

Late at night, in a forest of static,
I stumble on Radio Prague,

just as it follows Handel's Water Music
with crackling 30s cabaret,

and then The BeeGees, and the lights
all going out in Massachusetts...

Luxembourg, or Radio Free Europe,
throws in a chunk of rock.

And then, on another, stranger channel,
I can just make out my father

telling old stories of his crystal sets:
a boy under the bedclothes;

accented, urgent English, almost inaudible,
and Hungary, Hungary calling...

## *Radio Free Nowhere*

We broadcast on the move,
one day perhaps from an attic
in a derelict terrace,
the next from an old shed
on a disused allotment.

We can set up shop anywhere
and be gone in an hour
leaving things as we found them.
The only risk we run
is to be caught in the act,

our transmissions so short,
so nearly untraceable,
a poem or a manifesto
sandwiched between records
is almost unnoticeable,

its small infiltration lodged
in any ear close to a set
a hair's-breadth of ore
or a fleck of mica
in their acres of soft rock.

HOWARD TESSLER

*Scenario for an untuned grave*

One day
I will die
and become
a Phd dissertation topic.

Some hot shot
26 year old from Mississauga
will go backward
through my poetry;
confuse my metaphors
for symbols
and wax philosophic
over my line breaks.

He will conclude
"Here is a poet
who deserves the serious attention
of all students
of Canadian Literature."

Adding good manure
to my grave
the worms will be happy
for all his erudition.

I'll be quiet of course:
I'm dead
and will refuse to comment
on the delightful situation.

But one day
when this hot shot
is romancing some 18 year old
with a great ass and no taste
the bartender will lean over,
pour them each a stiff one
and say
"Hey Mister.  That ain't no metaphor.
That's my mother you're talking about.
So shut your face.
Sir."
The hot shot will smile
nervously
and three worms
will go deaf
from my laughter.

ANN CIMON

## Dream: In Flight

Last night I dreamt I was flying.
I, so fearful of airplanes
was strapped in a seat
and the window popped open
and in a panic I called the steward
who arrived with an olive
skewered to a toothpick
and assured me this would do the trick, and
I thought: why do some people always think
they have the answer to my problem?

*Driving Patterns*

Hilda and Wesley, driving. Hilda behind the wheel, envies the truckers she sees on the road. She envies them their freedom, their powerful vehicles. She gives the car some gas, and the Chrysler, towing an *Odysseus* camper, glides into the passing lane and sweeps past an eighteen wheeler. Hilda glances up at the driver; he has a red, beefy face, with sideburns the red-gold of desert sand. If I was alone, Hilda thinks, I'd get myself a CB radio, though I don't know how I'd learn to tune in the truckers' channels. She thinks on that for a while, decides she would go to a radio store, appear helpless, say she was buying the unit as a surprise for her husband who trucked all the way from Iowa to Georgia and back. Yes, that's what she'd do. See how that hand played.

For a while she fantasized about the golden-haired trucker. Hilda and Wesley are an hour out of Cheyenne, heading toward Billings, and eventually for Banff National Park and the Rocky Mountains. Hilda's professionally lightened hair is the color of a canary. Her body, sturdy as a sack of corn, is covered in a Carribean-blue, Fortrel pantsuit. She wishes she was young enough to be attractive to the truck driver. She wishes she was not fifty-two. She wishes she was alone in the car. Such thoughts make her feel guilty. She looks over at Wesley, who is sitting against the far door, a white tee-shirt covering his pigeon chest. Wesley is reading from a paperback book, his voice a soothing monotone. He is wearing a pair of lemon-colored slacks, brown loafers, and has a self-satisfied expression on his bland face. Hilda wants to do something to shake Wesley up. She lets the car wander over the center line, keeping one eye on Wesley as she does so. He waits a long time before he says anything, but he raises himself higher on his seat, his head closer to the windshield. Hilda is pleased to see that there is genuine fear on his face.

"What are you do. . . " he starts, but at the first sound of his voice Hilda guides the car back to the proper lane, the oncoming traffic still not dangerously close.

"Don't get all excited," Hilda says, as if she is admonishing a child. Her features are calm, but inwardly she is smiling. This is the third time in three days she has scared Wesley. "Why don't you keep on reading to me?" she says conversationally. Wesley reaches toward the dash and picks up the novel he set down when she let the car wander. The novel tells the story of a senator who is trying to overthrow the President.

Until they retired, Hilda had scarcely driven in her life, although she had always had access to a car, and occasionally drove her daughter, Lorraine, to school, or into Postville to 4-H, Girl Scouts, or something like that. When she and Wesley started traveling, Hilda suddenly discovered that she felt in control behind the wheel of the car. She quickly grew to like the feeling.

63

Hilda had been raised in McGregor, Iowa, a dying town on the Mississippi River, near the Wisconsin border. After high school, she had gone to Chicago and taken a job with a large insurance company. She sat all day in an artificially lighted room with forty other young women, typing case histories. She lived alone in a tiny basement suite in a nice residential district. She put up lemon-drop curtains, and painted and polished and decorated.

"When you meet a nice boy, your apartment will let him know right off that you're a homemaker," her mother had told her.

As they drive, Hilda tunes out Wesley's reading voice. Hilda thinks again of the truck driver, decides that she has had only one truly exciting day in her entire life: June 6, 1952.

She was already engaged to Wesley; in fact he was driving to Chicago to be with her that weekend. On her way home from work, she got off the bus at her regular stop, but as she approached a small grocery store she noticed a magnificient candy-apple-red motorcycle angle parked at the curb. When she was a few feet from the cycle its owner appeared. He was a tall young man with shaggy blond hair, a fierce face with wide-set eyes, and a large, sensual mouth. Hilda had actually broken stride to stare at the young man as he casually mounted the motorcycle. As she continued down the street she turned not once, but several times, to stare at him. She heard the bike roar to life, and as she turned once more, the cycle cruised into the curb beside her. The owner smiled and signalled her to climb on behind him. He was dressed all in denim, the back of his jacket was covered in red and black designs and lettering. Almost in a trance, Hilda complied. The bike idled for a moment.

"Put your arms around me and hang on," the driver said.

Again Hilda did as she was told. She pressed her face against the back of his jacket which smelled of fresh air, grease, and something spicy. He took her about a mile away to where he lived in a junky old house with orange dogs sleeping on the porch.

They scarcely exchanged a word as they made love all evening in his cluttered room. Hilda had a number of sexual experiences that evening which were completely new to her, experiences which were not even mentioned covertly in *A Teenager's Guide to Love and Marriage*, which she had received as a Christmas gift the year she turned seventeen. The young man took control so easily. Hilda envied him his ease and expertise. She and Wesley considered themselves daring for making love on the weekends he drove to Chicago. But what they did was sudden and awkward, inhibited by clothes and contraceptives.

In the days following the interlude with the boy on the motorcycle, Hilda was both thrilled and horrified by what she had done. In bed with the biker she had been positively acrobatic; she was sore in a number of places for several days. Hilda was sorry that she had no truly close girlfriends in whom to confide her wickedness. When she called her mother she joked about being sore, blaming it on rearranging furniture. Alone, she fantasized permanent injury, infection, disease, pregnancy. All the old wives' tales she had ever heard festered in her head. She checked herself several times a day for vaginal discharge.

That weekend, as soon as Wesley arrived they made frantic love between the crisp sheets of her single bed with its rose-colored satin spread. Afterwards, Wesley was jocular and self-satisfied, thinking he had been responsible for her passion.

Hilda had seen the cyclist on one other occasion, but he had not seen her. As she was walking downtown, a few months later, she noticed him pull up across the street, parking in front of a rather sleazy bar called The Logjam. Behind him, on the candy-appled bike, rode a slim young woman with curly, black hair. The woman was dressed in denim and wore motorcycle boots.

Hilda looked down at herself, at the polka dot print dress she wore, and the white platform shoes with the yellow-daisy fasteners. She tried to picture herself in denim and boots, walking into the rancid-smelling bar on the biker's arm. But she could not.


At first they took turns driving fifty miles each. Whoever finished up at night did not start in the morning. The first summer they even kept a little log book showing how far they traveled each day and who drove each portion of the journey. When Wesley was at the wheel, Hilda secretly hoped that he would drive on and on. When she knew it was nearly her turn to drive, Hilda would start a new chapter in whatever book they were reading aloud. The freeways were worrisome; the other drivers went too fast; it seemed to Hilda that truckers liked to ride on her bumper.

But, gradually, she gained confidence. The air conditioned Chrysler padded softly as a cat down the highways. She ceased to be surprised and nervous when she sighted the camper in the side-view mirror. She became expert at backing in and out of parking spaces. Sometimes she forgot entirely about the driving and let her mind wander away from Wesley's voice, away from the car, and back years and years to her one moment of what might have been.

It was through her mother that she met Wesley. She came home for a weekend her first October in Chicago, and went to church with her parents. They attended Trinity Episcopal, and were, like most Episcopalians, rather casual about their religion. Wesley was a nephew of someone in the congregation, an earnest young man in a sport jacket that fitted poorly.

During all their married years Hilda and Wesley never attended church. Once, early in the marriage, when she had suggested it, Wesley replied: "I only went to church so I could meet a good girl."

Wesley was red-complexioned with a sloping forehead and chin, and eyebrows the color of corn silk. He farmed with his father on two sections of prime land near Postville, a few miles west of McGregor. His parents were preparing to retire, and the deal was struck that Wesley would farm the land, split the income with them during their lifetimes, and inherit the land after they were gone. Anything the parents saved from their half would go to Wesley's sister, who was five years older and married to a bank manager in Cedar Falls.

Hilda and Wesley had one daughter, Lorraine, who was agreeable and obedient, and who was in her final year of law school at Drake University in Des Moines when Wesley decided to retire. Lorraine was now graduated and working for the Peace Corps.

Wesley announced his retirement on his fiftieth birthday.

"I want to travel," he said. "I want to see the United States."

The announcement caught Hilda by surprise. I'm not old enough to retire, she thought. Won't everyone consider us old if we're retired? She equated retirement with death. Her few friends told her how lucky she was, most of their husbands were workaholics, they said.

The first summer on the road, Hilda saw more parks, cairns, and museums than she dreamed existed. Wesley began keeping a diary, listing meticulously, like an accountant, all the places they visited. We're drifting across the surface of the United States, Hilda thought. We're like those long-legged insects that glide over placid water, walking so lightly they don't disturb the surface.

The farm had brought an exorbitant price. They were financially secure. After traveling until October, they returned to Postville, where they rented a one-bedroom apartment with a fireplace which was equipped with glass doors, where they burned colored logs as they spent the winter days watching a super-sized television.

It was during the second summer on the road that their driving patterns began to change. When she was the driver, Hilda began locking her door. She had heard on *Donahue* that most drivers who were injured in accidents were thrown from the vehicle on impact.

Hilda tried to imagine what it would be like to be dead. I haven't even begun to live, she thought. My life hasn't started. It's as if I've lived in a cocoon all these years. Most people consider us lucky and rich in everything. We've had no tragedies, no failures. But there's been no happiness. No real successes. We've drifted. Having nothing happen to you isn't necessarily living.

"What are we going to do?" Hilda asked Wesley, as they floated along the California coast highway in the Big Sur, high above the foggy ocean with its dark rocks, and cavorting seals.

"About what?"

"About us," she replied.

"I thought we were happy," said Wesley.

"I didn't say I wasn't," said Hilda. "What I said was, 'What are we going to do?' Are we going to spend the rest of our lives skimming along highways in the summer and hibernating in the winter?"

"If you're unhappy, we can do anything you want to do. What would you like to do?"

But Hilda couldn't think of anything she wanted to do, except go back to 1952 and start all over again.


"I feel like driving a hundred miles," Hilda announced one day during the second summer. Wesley looked up from the book he was reading. Hilda listened sporadically to the books Wesley read; he listened intently when she read aloud, often asking her to repeat a passage or scene. Wesley bought the books; always adventure novels, political thrillers, mysteries. The one they were currently reading was about a U.S. President who sells out to the Russians, and the Dallas newspaper reporter who was the only person in the world who could stop the sellout.

Hilda drove one hundred and fifty miles. Wesley drove fifty. Hilda then drove for the rest of the day.

In San Francisco she went to a book store and bought several hardcover works of fiction, after asking the advice of the wise-looking book store owner. "Challenging" was the word he used to describe her choices.

But as Wesley droned on from a new book, Hilda's mind continued to float away; she could not follow the stories, there was too much rumination. Navel-gazing, Wesley called it. And too much obscenity. It embarrassed Wesley to read sexually explicit passages.

Maybe if I pretend I've been *that* girl, Hilda thinks. Where would I be now? You don't see couples over thirty riding around on motorcycles. Do those men die young? Or do they just get worn down by life like everybody else, and end up as watchmen or janitors, living in two-room rented apartments in small towns? What became of that girl with the black, curly hair, sitting so jauntily on the motorcycle, smoking a cigarette? What becomes of young women like that? Where do they go? Do they become those gaunt women with ravaged faces who sit in taverns, make-up slurred, voices quarrelsome?

Living without passion is the worst thing a person can let happen to herself, Hilda thinks. She eyes Wesley, who reads on, half smiling.

In April, when they started their third year on the road, Hilda began fastening her seatbelt. She also began doing all the driving. She took the first turn in the morning, driving about a hundred miles, and, after they stopped for coffee, she would say cheerfully, "I enjoy driving. I'll keep on if you don't mind."

For the first few days Wesley continued to offer to take his turn.

"But I don't mind driving," Hilda would say. "It makes me feel useful. Besides, you read so much better than I do." Wesley would acquiesce, smiling his self-satisfied smile, hauling the current novel up from the floor on his side of the car.

Besides feeling that she has somehow missed out entirely on life, Hilda feels that as she has grown older she has become solider, not just physically, but more visible. She has gained substance, she thinks, while Wesley has lost substance, has faded like one of the black velvet cushions that used to sit on their sofa on the farm. The sun faded the black velvet to the color of dust, the bright oranges and reds of the punchwork flowers to a uniform cream color. Hilda remembers working Saturdays during high school at an old fashioned Woolworth's, with dark counters, the whole store smelling of baking donuts. Remembering the store, she realizes that she has come to think of Wesley as one of those pale, transluscent fish that used to sit languidly in the greeny aquarium water at Woolworth's. The boy on the motorcycle she thinks of as one of the plump, black fish with protruding eyes, aggressive, full of danger.

At an entrance ramp to I-15, near Great Falls, Montana, Hilda pulls into traffic too soon and too slowly. On her bumper, a trucker sounds his foghorn-like horn.

"Watch out!" cries Wesley.

"Don't be so grouchy," Hilda yells at the truck as it growls around them. "If I had a CB, I'd give that fellow a good earful."

"You were at fault," says Wesley.

"He was speeding," says Hilda sullenly.

She makes herself comfortable behind the wheel of the Chrysler, pats her lemon-colored hair, checks the rearview. It will be a long day.

"I sure wouldn't mind hearing a chapter of that book," she says, making her voice cheery, congenial.

They spend the night in a quiet, mom and pop motel and trailer park near the Canadian border. Over breakfast Hilda maps out their route, using a vermilion-colored felt marker to widen the road until it looks like a river of blood on the map.

Wesley begins reading as soon as they are gliding along the interstate. He bought a western novel in Billings: an evil land baron is bringing in a hired gunslinger to keep the homesteaders in line.

Hilda has a vent open so the wind blows full onto her face. She steers the car with her fingertips, wheeling it into the passing lane and zooming around a semitrailer. She breathes deeply, experiencing the wind in her face, the power of the cycle between her thighs, the muffler snarling as she feeds gas to the engine. The boy from long ago sits behind her now, his strong arms clenched securely around her. She presses the accelerator. Beside her, as if obscured by the blur of speed and blue-tinted glass, Wesley

68

drones on, sunning himself. Hilda increases speed, the roar of the cycle fills her ears. She envisions winding mountain roads.

Eyes fastened to the book, staring neither right nor left, placid and self-satisfied, Wesley turns himself slightly in Hilda's direction, adjusting his posture in the death seat.

SU CROLL

*Pushed Up By Easter*

My father is the only person
who is not afraid to die
It's something you have to plan for
pushing the bulbs down
and giving them enough cover
There already was a christ
and nobody wants to admit they need
another one   Our own house
is the fuel of it and we burn
ourselves to keep warm
And who is not afraid of dying?
As though they all had cold hands
and the hearts of blue eyed dogs
Lost in the country that is most familiar
My own grandmother pushed up
by Easter

## Katherine

That Katherine
she never went in for blood sports
cringes and runs for chapel
at the first sound of the hunting horn

But every night she braves it in the bear pit
with that pit bull of a husband of hers

You know she's tough as nails
and she's been filled up and emptied out
more than once
Every year
the royal physician sneaking out the slop jar of royal blood pudding
and the terrified midwives
taking that blood 'n' bread pie out to bury by the river

That Katherine
when she died
they dug out her blackened heart with a silver teaspoon
I leaned over and watched

Now it's my turn
I grit my teeth with Hal trying to force all of his England into me
grunting like a hungry bull dog
and thinking he can fill me up with sons

ALEXANDER HUTCHISON

*Surprise, Surprise*

McSween the corner butcher with confidence displays
for denizens of the city — 'of toons the *a per se*' —
a vegetarian haggis, rank specimen of his craft.
Just what the creature might contain defeats surmise:
pinmeal and onions, nuts or beans, some dribs and drabs.
No gristle, no suet, no organ meats:  no liver, no tripes
no lights, no heart.  Instead of a sheep's paunch
potato skins with a saddle-stitch fly.  Up the Mound
down Candlemakers Row the fix is in.  The *makars* jump
the peddlers stump, the market splits wide open.

First *from a purely culinary point of view* — corned, curried
devilled, smoked and kosher haggis; haggis a la king; wee cocktail
haggis; haggis in a basket; haggis on the half shell; *instant* haggis;
*English* haggis; haggis eclairs; Crimean campaign haggis, conceived
in Sebastopol, consumed in Balaclava; hot-cross haggis; haggis in
plum sauce; dessicated haggis; baked haggis alaska; chocolate mint-
chip haggis; non-stick convenient haggis; cucumber and haggis
sandwiches; junk haggis; whole-hog haggis.

Next *by haggis of a special bent* — weight-watcher haggis;
haggis for the moonstruck; haggis *nouveau*; haggis *gran cru*; 12 year
old vintage haggis matured in oak casks; 100 year old Kung Po haggis
drawn from the well without obstruction; "Bomber" Haggis; haggis for
lovers; lite lo-tar, lo-nicotine haggis; Campdown haggis; drive-in
haggis; hand-raised, house-trained haggis, with pedigree attached;
haggis by special appointment; reconstituted haggis; nuclear-free
haggis; ancient Dynastic haggis sealed in canopic jars; haggis
quickstep; haggis high in fibre; haggis low in the opinion of several
discerning people; a haggis of the Queen's flight; Nepalese temple
haggis (rich, dark and mildew-free); hard-porn haggis; haggis
built to last.

Finally *objects tending to the metaphysical* — desolation
haggis; the canny man's haggis; haggis not so good or bad as
one imagines; haggis made much of caught young; unsung haggis;
haggis not of this fold; haggis dimm'd by superstition;
perfectly intuited haggis; haggis beyond the shadow of a doubt;
bantering haggis; haggis given up for Lent; haggis given up for
lost; haggis so good you think you died and went to heaven;
haggis supreme; haggis unchained.

## *The Chain*

Martine lay in the brass bed, staring at the clock on the table across the room. It was her husband's little alarm clock and she kept it dutifully wound although it had recently gone berserk and was next to useless. It was on a sort of rampage and gained twenty minutes every hour. Right now she could hear it ticking away at breakneck speed. She squinted at the dial — it said twenty past three. But she knew it couldn't be much after ten.

It came back to her suddenly that she'd been jolted awake this morning at dawn, after three hours of sleep, by a noise which seemed to come from somewhere in the house. It had sounded like Gordon's voice. Of course, Gordon was thousands of miles away. But she thought she'd heard him say her name quite distinctly. She'd lain there listening, her heart pounding, half-expecting him to burst in on her and Peter, but of course it had only been a dream of some kind.

Martine liked the mornings; sometimes she almost felt like jumping out of bed and running here and there, like the chickens. But what was there for a human being to do at that hour? After all, she was not a Greek housewife with children to feed and floors to scrub. So she would lie sometimes, at dawn, open-eyed, watching the window, as the sky turned from grey to pearl to brilliant blue. Afterwards she would fall into a heavy, drugged sleep from which she would wake, puffy-eyed and sweating, sometime before noon. She was not yet used to the Greek schedule, which was based on early rising and late bedtimes, with a siesta in the afternoon to make up the difference.

But now she heard the clock chiming down in the port — nine, ten, eleven. Eleven. She still had time to get to the post office before everything closed for siesta.

She slipped out of bed and went to the garden, where a hose was lying coiled around a metal faucet. The sun had heated the water in the hose and she splashed some on her face and stood under it for a few seconds, to dissolve some of the stickiness.

She tiptoed back into the bedroom and found the wrinkled white dress she had thrown on the chair the night before. She put it on and brushed her hair. She didn't feel inclined to wake Peter — he liked his sleep. He was sprawled on the bed like a squashed grasshopper, legs and arms at extravagant angles, snoring. His white straw hat was on the bedpost where he had placed it last night, when he delivered his strange bedtime lecture.

"The greatest gift a woman can have," he had told her, "is to be an inspiration to a man." He'd been offended when she laughed out loud.

"What's so funny about that?" he'd wanted to know.

73

"You sound just like my husband." That had shut him up for a moment. Perhaps she oughtn't to have referred to Gordon as 'my husband' — it made poor Peter uncomfortable.

She'd tried to make light of it, but that had only got him going. He'd released all the frustration built up from a week of profoundly unexceptional sex, and thrown it at her. She'd laughed, but underneath she was disappointed that he was so quickly becoming predictable.

Last night during their argument he had invoked his wife reflexively, in a moment of anger. "You're just like Virginia," he'd said, flinging it at her. "You don't know how to make a man happy!"

He'd looked like a child having a tantrum.

She'd said, "I'm sorry, but I am not your wife and you can't abuse me because I'm not chained to you, you know." But though she hid her feelings well, she was hurt by the things he had said. After all, she'd only got involved with Peter because he reminded her of her husband. Now she realized her mistake.

She had been waiting around now for over a month, and though Gordon sent her plenty of money to spend on herself, she was bored, terribly bored. She was waiting for a letter from him, but he never wrote. He simply expected her to wait, on this island, with these strangers who all claimed to be his friends. Apparently he thought a woman should be able to wait indefinitely. Early June, he'd promised, and now it was almost July. The time for their vacation together was slipping by. What could he be doing that was taking so long? Business, he'd said, vaguely, but that had only convinced her he was seeing someone else.

And (what was almost worse) other people thought so too. A week hardly went by without someone making some biting little remark. "Where's Gordon?" they would ask. She felt more than a little resentful of him. Some of his 'friends' actually seemed to look down on her, as though she were a scrap of something that had been blown here by the wind. She didn't like to think of herself as pathetic, but apparently there were people who thought of her that way.

She couldn't be expected to take care of everything herself. Already things at the house were falling apart. The fleas in the middle room were getting out of control.

And nobody'd warned her about the red ants, small enough to slip into the refrigerator through a gap in the insulation around the door. For a week now they'd been coming in a steady stream, from the back door to the fridge and back again out the door. Now and then she got out a wet rag and wiped them up, washing them down the kitchen drain with water from the pitcher. She also wiped them out of the fridge, their drowned bodies floating in the vegetable bin.

Sometimes when she couldn't stand the insects and the boredom at Gordon's, she went to see Peter. Peter owned a house overlooking the

74

beach. He'd bought it with money he'd made dealing on the commodities market. But in 'real life', he told her, he was an artist.

"Would you like to see my work?" he'd asked her, the first time she visited him. He'd led her upstairs to an empty room with an improvised table in one corner, littered with brushes and tiny watercolours. He showed her a hundred photos he had recently taken, all of rocks, except for one — of his wife. She had a glittering smile and hard little eyes.

"We're getting divorced," he said. "She lives in France. It took me only six months to realize I should never have married her."

He shook his head, letting her photograph fall on the table.

"She's bad for my art," he concluded, as if that were the ultimate outrage.

They'd sat in his kitchen, where spiders were building webs in the hanging pots and pans, and in every available corner of the cupboards. These spiders were a large variety, with yellow egg sacs as big as grapes.

"Why don't you kill them?" she'd asked, looking around with distaste.

"Motherhood is sacred here," said Peter. "And anyway, they're harmless. They only eat flies."

Not kill them: she'd never heard of anything so stupid. But it wasn't her job to do it.

Now in the light of day it seemed absurd that she was involved with Peter. He might have money, but what, after all, was money if he were crazy? She dismissed him from her mind and unlocked the gate, trying not to see the starving family of cats who watched her without hope from their patch of shade near the garden wall. "Don't feed them," Peter had warned her. "If you do you'll never get rid of them."

It was not yet noon but the heat was already overpowering. She wished she knew how to find the shortcut to the port that Peter had showed her two days ago. As it was she took the usual route, which was circuitous and offered little shelter from the sun.

The cicadas were scraping and sawing up in the eucalyptus trees. They would go on all day, like mad violinists whom no one could silence. It was the heat, she thought, that pulled time out of shape. Sometimes she felt it was affecting her mind.

At this hour the air was wavy with the heat and the streets glowed white. The houses looked like skeleton's teeth studding the hillside. The land had baked brown, and corpses of spring flowers lay like straw beside the donkeypath. Chickens scratched listlessly in the dirt beside kitchen doors. Whole families of cats were starving to death all over the island, and Martine hated passing them on her way into town, hearing their plaintive meows.

She arrived in the little square where the post office was. Some Japanese tourists were taking turns photographing each other next to the handicraft stall which stood across from a souvlaki place and the public toilets.

She climbed the steps of the post office. Inside, it was cool and dark and several people were standing in line for their mail. When she reached the front of the line, Martine gave her name, and was pleased when the girl handed her an envelope. If it were more money from Gordon, she would buy herself a dress to cheer herself up.

She tore it open and read:

"And He will acknowledge and He will light the Way."
This prayer has been sent to you for good luck, the original copy is from the Netherlands. It has been around the world nine times. The luck has been brought to you. You are to receive luck within four days of receiving this letter, and this is not a joke, you will receive it in the mail. Send copies of this letter to people you think will need good luck. DO NOT SEND MONEY.

An RAP officer received $10,000. Don Elliott received $50,000 and lost it because he broke the chain. While in the Philippines, General Welch lost his life 6 days after he received this letter. He failed to circulate the prayer. However, before his death he received $775,000. Please send 20 copies and see what happens to you on the fourth day. This chain comes from Venezuela and was written by Sol Anthony c/r CADIF a missionary from South America. Since this chain must make a tour of the world, you must make 20 copies identical to this and send it to your friends, parents and acquaintances. After a few days you will get a surprise. This is true even if you are not superstitious. Take a note to the following:

Constantine Dine received this chain in 1953. He asked his secretary to make 20 copies and send them. A few days later he won a lottery of 20 million dollars. In this country, Charles Cradvit, an office employee received the chain. He forgot about it and subsequently lost his job. He found it and sent it to 20 people, 5 days later he got an even better job. Colin Meinchild received the chain and not believing in it threw it away and 9 days later died.

For no reason whatsoever can this chain be broken.

DO NOT SEND MONEY

There was no signature on the letter, and no return address. So she had come all the way down here for a chain letter! She tore the envelope in half and threw it into the waste basket. But she stuffed the letter into her pocket. There was something about it. She would take it along to the bar tonight, and read it aloud to the others. It might amuse them. People here were desperate for any sort of distraction.

She went and had a look around the village square, but saw no one she knew. Somewhere just behind her, the clock tower had begun chiming its little noonhour tune. In a moment those final, deafening twelve strokes would begin, overpowering all other sounds in the port. Martine sank into a chair, next to a statue of a man seated on a lion — some hero of the War of Independence. The loud monotonous bonging began and her mind went suddenly blank. She covered her eyes for a moment, allowing herself to disappear. When she looked up a waiter was looming over her, holding a round silver tray. "Se parakalo?"

"I'd like a coffee please, with cream."

The waiter spun around and shouted to someone inside the restaurant: "Ena nescafe, meh gala!"

She blinked and gazed around the port. Over by the ticketseller's, a blue and yellow hydrofoil was gliding into dock, and people were crowding round to board it, or to meet the passengers who had taken it from Athens.

What if Gordon were on that boat, she thought, trying to imagine it. For an instant she had a clear image of him, stern and dignified, stepping out onto the gangplank. She fingered the gold chain round her neck — a gift when he'd proposed to her last year, at the height of their affair.

The waiter was back again with his tray and her coffee, that horrible instant stuff they served everywhere in Greece. She hoped the cream at least would not be rancid. It came to 22 drachmas. She paid and looked over her shoulder at the hydrofoil, which was pulling out of the harbour now, in a cloud of blue-grey diesel smoke.

She sank back in the plastic chair, closing her eyes, and gave herself up to the heat. When she opened them, a young man was sitting in the seat opposite.

"Luc," she said. "You awful boy. How long have you been sitting there?"

He shrugged and looked over his shoulder, trying to get the waiter's attention.

"So," he said, twisting himself round again, one arm dangling from the chairback, "where is your husband?"

"I wonder." She smiled at him, her eyes widening. He was handsomer than Peter. Brown eyes. Sensual body. Perfectly modelled face.

He made a knowing little sideways movement of the head. "Poor Gordon is a busy man. A very important man." His soft lips parted in a smile. He was looking at her intently.

77

He waved at the waiter. "You'll buy me a cappuccino?" he said to her.

"Of course."

"Cappuccino and a glass of water."

He leaned forward, stretching out his legs and staring into her face. "I have some photographs I would like you to look at. They are at my house. Are you busy this afternoon? Once you've seen them everything you read in books will be nothing but a caption."

"They sound very interesting," she said.

"Come for supper around six. You know the house? It's the one next to the red Church, just above Marigoula's store."

"I think I can find it."

He finished his coffee and stood up. "See you," he said. He formed the words like a kiss.


From Luc's terrace, the whole of the harbour was clearly visible, but in miniature. People were approximately the size of ants. They still had human shapes, but without identity, without personality. She wished she had a spyglass so she could observe what they were doing, the way she'd observed the lives of ants as a child.

Luc came out of the kitchen, carrying a tray with tea. Up here there were no neighbours; no one could see them sitting on the terrace, and yet from her position she could see what was going on a quarter of a mile down the hill.

He put down the tray with the cups and spoons. "Here are the photographs," he said, pointing to an envelope on the table.

He filled two cups and handed her one of them. She looked at the first photograph. It was of a beautiful young man, naked, chained to a tree. Another man stood next to him, holding a whip.

"You may find them difficult to understand," said Luc. "I was more than myself when they were taken." He looked away down the hillside.

She sipped her tea and looked at them, one by one. "I think they're...," she said. She followed his gaze down to the harbour, where another hydrofoil was coming in to dock. She suddenly wished Gordon to be on it.

"What's wrong?" he said. "Shocked?"

He pulled her to her feet and kissed her. Then he stood looking down at the harbour.

"I feel something strange is happening to me," he said. "I have the feeling there is something wrong with my life, as if I were one of the damned."

She laughed. "Now you're getting melodramatic."

"You remember that lightning storm a few weeks ago? You know which house was struck?"

"This one."

"Of all the houses on the island! Me, I'd gone to bed drunk. I didn't even wake up. But the next morning when I went down to the kitchen I saw that the fuse box was black, and all the wires had burned to a powder. It must have been a real explosion."

Martine listened, smiling. "Maybe it happened because you've been chosen."

"Chosen?"

"I was just joking," she said quickly.

"Do you think I am a destructive force?" he asked. Then he laughed.

She felt far away suddenly. She turned to look at the sea. The noise of the cicadas filled her ears.

"That reminds me of something." She reached in her pocket and pulled out the chain letter.

"Listen to this," she said. "Under no circumstances can this chain be broken."

"What's that?"

"It's a chain letter. Listen: ...And nine days later died." The phrase sounded ominous to her. "I think my husband sent it."

"Why?"

"As a joke, maybe. To frighten me."

"Your husband is thousands of miles away."

"But what if it were true?"

"If what were true?" He stepped forward and embraced her, slipping his hand down between her legs, applying pressure. "Your body is the only reality," he said. "The mind is just a machine. This is what I have learned, through those photographs. An experience... If it were possible now, I would show you..."

She looked down at the ground near her foot, where three large black ants were dragging something away. She leaned closer to see what it was. They were humpbacked ants with enormous jaws. Three of them circling around the prize. Sometimes all together they tried to lift the thing but it was too heavy and awkward for them. It was the head and beak of a newborn baby bird.

She looked again. It was pink, almost transparent, a few hours old. For a moment it had lived, and now the undertakers were already hauling it away.

From over Luc's shoulder she could see the other, distant ant-world down in the port.

"And even if he were one of those little shapes down there, stepping off the boat, from up here I'd never know it. It wouldn't make any difference."

That evening Martine and Luc went drinking in the port. She read her chain letter aloud to a group of Gordon's friends, but nobody laughed.

"Let's go to another place," she said. "I find these people unbearable."

At the next bar, they ran into Peter, but Martine ostentatiously ignored him and he left with another girl a little after midnight. Soon afterwards she also left, with Luc.

"This is an awful place," she said, as they staggered up the hill.

"It's not awful if you don't think about it," said Luc.

He was delicately, fragrantly drunk, and balanced himself in his drunkeness like a dancer. On the stone bridge over the dried-up riverbed, he swayed for a moment, admiring the moonlight.

"Before you can create something," he said, "something has to be destroyed. I have always wanted to be a hero..." He pressed her to the stone wall of the bridge, leaning his full weight against her.

"C'est ton corps," he said, "ton corps..."

His room was like a cave, utterly simple, a camping space with a kerosene lamp, a few books. There was a patchwork quilt on the bed, and the sheets underneath were yellowish. As she undressed she looked around the room, at the hotplate in the corner, the cigarette butts on the floor. She unclasped the silver chain from her neck and put it on the table beside the bed.

They slept under the crazy quilt, a candle flickering on the table beside the bed. Tiny insects bit them and kept them awake almost till dawn. Luc made love to her several times; she lost count, or stopped caring. It was sometimes almost painful, but in a way that she knew was painful to them both. She felt their bodies were growing roots in each other. She imagined this was love; love without personality.

She dreamed that Gordon came to her and congratulated her, handing her a card with the word 'Leukemia' written on it.

She woke up trembling in the bed, soaked with sweat. She felt for the chain around her neck but of course it was gone. She couldn't remember what she'd done with it.

Luc stirred beside her. It was just before dawn. For the first time in her life she felt she was seeing things as they actually were. Her heart pounded and her skin felt like a frail envelope, transparent. At any moment it might burst. In the distance a rooster was screaming but there was a great stillness in her ears, and her life seemed to hang above her like something apart and senseless.

*below the belt*

"that boy
I declare
every time he gets his self into a fight
he gets beat up

never does win nothin

and then he gets all swoll up
eyes black an blued
and comes home
and wants me to take care of him

so even though he's thirty-three now
I just gets out that old ice pack
like I done when he was a kid
and had the mumps
and old Doc Songer was tellin me
what to do

why I just fills up that bag
with ice cubes

and packs his balls
till the swelling goes down

but I declare
it's surely gettin
hard to keep
that pack
on him
nowadays"

LEONARD COHEN

## *When Even The*

Your breasts are like.
Your thighs and your carriage.
I never thought.
Somewhere there must be.
It's possible.
Summer has nothing.
Even Spring doesn't.
Your feet are so.
It's cruel to.
My defense is.
Summer certainly doesn't.
Your.
And your.
If only.
Somewhere there must.

        But the.
        And the.
        It's enough to.
        Soldiers don't.
        Prisoners don't.
        Maybe the turtle.
        Maybe hieroglyphics.
        Sand.
        But in your cold.
        If I could.
        If once more.
        Slip or liquid.
        But the.
        And the.

Sometimes when.
Even tho'.
Yes even tho'.
They say suffering.
They say.
Okay then let's.
Let's.
The sign is.
The seal is.
The guarantee.
Oh but.

O cruel.
O blouse with.
This is what.
And why it isn't.

　　　　　But what do they.
　　　　　What do they.
　　　　　When even.
　　　　　When even the.
　　　　　Years will.
　　　　　Death will.
　　　　　But they won't.
　　　　　Even if.
　　　　　Even if the.
　　　　　They never will.

O deceiver.
O deceptive.
Turn your eyes.
Incline your.
To the one who.
Rotten as.
Hungry as.
Who does not.
Who never will.
But now your.
And your.
And these arms.
Which is lawless.
Which is blind.
If you come.
If you find.
Then I.

　　　　　Like all.
　　　　　Like every.
　　　　　　　　　　If only.
　　　　　　　　　　If when.
　　　　　Even though.
　　　　　Even if.
　　　　　　　　　　Not for.
　　　　　　　　　　Not for.
　　　　　But only.
　　　　　But every.

83

LEONARD COHEN

If I could.
When the.
Then I.
Even if.
Even when.
I would.

## *Art Roebuck Comes to* Born With A Tooth

Let us compare mythologies
Leonard Cohen

Years later when the acrid smoke of poplar roots stung her nostrils in the Buffalo Plains churchyard, after all the inexplicable changes to befall her family and the municipality of Born With A Tooth, Ida Cole would long since have forgotten the dream she'd had the day of the chickencoop: from the river's edge a fat brown and white goose comes to feed on grain beside the housetrailer, then a hook-beaked eagle swoops down from the TV antenna and breaks the goose's neck. "Ah say, be glad!" roars the bird. "Be glad, ah say, and weep not, for your lord and master is home." When she awoke she was digging her fingernails into her husband's arm.

Ida clenches a clothespin between her teeth and drapes a sheet over the line. Her four-year-old son plays nearby.

Deep in their sockets blaze eyes the colour of hazelnuts. Hot morning sun illuminates a corona of tiny white hairs on the boy's cheeks and ears as he sits splay-legged next to the rusted metal wheel of a gas wagon. Auburn in the aluminum sheen of the gastank, the brushcut hair outlines a broad white forehead and hollow temples that could have been squeezed by heavy fingers too soon after birth.

A canning sealer beside the boy's knee is clouded with brown grasshoppers who climb over one another's backs and heads, sliding down the jar's smooth sides as they struggle for a triangle of airholes punched in the tin lid. The boy screws off the ring. He holds the inner lid in place and shakes the jar up and down until the grasshoppers lie in a tangled knot on the glass floor. He lifts the tin disc, snatches a leg and snaps the top on before the others can escape. The boy dunks the insect headfirst into a pitcher of motor oil.

"Our Father, who ark in heaven,
Howled be thy name."

He pulls the grasshopper from the oil pitcher and releases it. "Two really big jumps, a pretty big jump, then a little jump." The grasshopper sits glistening on the hard white dirt where the tractor parks to get gassed up.

The boy takes another grasshopper from the jar.

"Our Father, who ark in heaven,
Howled be thy name.

Thy king does come. Thy will be done

8 5

On earth, as it is in heaven.

"One really big jump and a pretty big jump. A quick drink makes them jump far, but the longer they drink, the less they jump before they stop and just sit there all shiny." Ida considers telling him to stop drowning the grasshoppers but in the end says nothing. The boy shakes the jar.

"Our Father, who ark in heaven,
Howled be thy name.

Thy king does come. Thy will be done
On earth, as sit is in heaven.

Give us this day our daily br—"

Suddenly a loud squawking erupts in the chickencoop.

"Hartland go chase that pup away from the chickens," says Ida, clipping a tea towel to the line.

He waits and watches a grasshopper make its leap. "One middle-size jump." A louder noise comes from the chickencoop, not a chicken noise.

"Get going now."

The boy scrambles to his feet and runs. Ida hangs a final facecloth, throws the clothespins in the laundry basket and follows.

The henhouse is quiet. The hens are sitting still in their roosts, none of them pecking in the wooden graintrough or squabbling over the waterbucket. In the middle of the coop the rooster, usually out following the hens around, has his beak pressed into the floorboards. Claws hooked inward, his left foot sticks up in the air, while the white feathers of his left wing are ruffled like mussed hair. Every few seconds the left leg twitches.

Her son is staring at the bird's head. He pinches the skin of the red crest. The boy's jaw muscles bulge in and out as he grinds his teeth. He flicks the head and winces as it flops to one side on the limp neck. A puddle of dark blood has seeped onto the gray floorslats.

Ida pushes him aside. "Get away from there."

Slowly she circles the rooster in a squat; she starts as she glimpses the pantlegs of her husband: palms pressed against crisp bird dung rosebuds on the windowsill, dry lips slightly parted, hazel eyes glazed and staring into the centre of the chickencoop. A red-orange splotch fills a corner of his right eyeball.

Ida's heart thuds. She moistens her throat and utters a cracked whisper: "James?" The man doesn't blink.

She stands frozen while her son steps closer and taps the bristly fingers clutching the windowsill. "D—d—d—ad?" He grabs a fistful of his father's oily blue pantleg and shakes it, making a soft snap like laundry in a breeze. The man bolts from the boy and lunges blindly to the centre of the room, nearly trampling the dead rooster. A low dry growl rattles in his throat as he stares vaguely in the direction of his son.

The boy clings to Ida's leg. Suddenly she kicks the dead rooster sprawling and wraps her husband's arm round her shoulder. The gray pup yips and jumps at their heels as they walk to the housetrailer.

        •       •       •

*A marine was killed today when a heavily-populated section of Beirut was destroyed in mortar fire. Twenty-one-year-old Franklin Miller, a farmboy from near Fredonia, North Dakota, was to have enrolled in North Idaho Veterinary College in September. An honours student and all-star basketball forward, Franklin is survived by his parents and older brother. Deaths from the attack are estimated in the hundreds.*

Ida stopped feeding her husband to change the TV channel. Even with a choice of forty-five stations she could never decide on anything she wanted to watch. Six months earlier when she was in the city getting the old black-and-white television repaired she had filled out an entry form. A week later a truck came creeping down the valley hill and a representative from Electrohome took a polaroid picture of Ida while two men installed a television satellite antenna outside the trailer. It still felt funny watching such a multitude of programs on the old blue-gray screen; an antiquated pair of rabbit-ears remained on top of the box, tinfoil snowballs crumpled onto the tips.

James rocked in the rocking chair, eyes dull as boiled eggs. He seemed unaware that his meal had been interrupted. Warren Putnam snored on the chesterfield, the dog asleep at his side. The housetrailer's small gas furnace made a soft 'whump' as it cut in.

*All right Frank, how do you think Tracy responded to this question: What are you most proud of about your husband? What do you think your wife is most proud of about you Frank?*

*Studio audience chuckles.*

*Probably when I became head of my department.*

*I'm sure she's proud of that achievement but that's not what came first to her mind. When we asked Tracy what she was most proud of about her husband...well it had something to do with your stamina.*

*Audience erupts with laughter.*

Ida spooned macaroni and cheese into James' mouth and scraped the creamy orange dribbles from the corners of his mouth. She was glad she'd taken such painstaking care of her husband's teeth since he'd lost his ability to care for himself. It meant she didn't have to mush everything up for him. And even though Warren was settled in permanently on the farm she never lost hope that James might one day start noticing things again and be able to talk and walk and do everything just like before the chickencoop incident. He'd be grateful for the way she'd nursed him during the past fourteen years.

If she were on the TV show with the other couples Ida knew she would have trouble finding something that made her proud of Warren. She was pregnant with Sarah by the time she realized he was just going to be another motionless body for her to look after. When he wasn't sleeping he was in the Buffalo Plains beer parlour throwing darts.

She knew in an instant what made her proud of James but she couldn't put it into words. It was in everything he did, like the way he used to tell the time by the sun, the way he could spend an entire day alone in an ice-fishing hut without getting lonely. It was in the way he had passed up big money from a gravel company that wanted to dig up the valley hillsides. "Who am I to destroy these hills," he said. "They're not mine. I'm borrowing them for a few years, then somebody else'll borrow them." It was in the way he had quietly and firmly put an end to the bullying of Etienne Beaudoin at a Buffalo Plains Sports Day shivaree.

Etienne Beaudoin was a wild-eyed trapper who had squatted in a scoop-roofed shanty near the beaver pond until he burned to death beating wet gunnysacks against his cabin one night when spontaneous combustion ignited some damp turnips in the old roothouse. The fire razed most of the valley including the old Cole homestead. James had always welcomed the grizzled Frenchman, who would appear at the house smelling of kerosene and ermineskins, always with some pretext for coming: the gift of a syrup-pail of rosehips or a warning that for two nights running he had observed an unearthly glow around the chimney flashing on the Coles' roof. He was a real pioneer, he said, an original trailbreaking, sodbusting, bushwhacking homesteader. He'd timberjacked lodgepoles in the Kootenays, catskinned deadfall in Peace River Country and chuckdriven smokewagons on the Shaganappi Circuit. He'd been a bushpilot in a Coppermine whiteout and gone snowblind on a Whitehorse trapline. It was he who had started the joke about the ice worm, he who had invented the corduroy road, he who had built the first Saskatchewan sodshack. He claimed to hear the nocturnal yips of coyote pups whose spirits were buried beneath the stonepile in the far corner of the valley, and one night he arrived with the yarn that, on the path from his place, he had come face-to-face with a gleaming-eyed man robed in white who catechized him in a patois of Algonquin and Jesuit Latin without moving his lips.

It was the year they stopped running the Bennet buggy races at the Sports Day. Too drunk and decrepit to defend himself, the old man was being pushed back and forth by a circle of drunks. He staggered like a clubbed moose.

"Why Etienne," said James in a clear loud voice, "don't you think a gentleman your age should find this sort of roughhousing a little undignified? I thought you were a bit more refined than that." The circle of hoodlums parted, James took Etienne's arm in his and calmly led the old man to the car.

Ida pushed the spoon towards James' mouth but his head moved sideways. This is new, she thought. He usually ate until she stopped feeding. There was a glimmer of expression in his eyes. Then she realized he was looking past her at the television. A girl in a bikini was chugging a Diet Pepsi. After the commercial James' eyes went back to normal. Ida snapped her fingers in front of his face and waved her hand back and forth but he didn't respond.

Entire weeks passed on the farm when no one spoke more than a couple of sentences. James had sat wordless in the rocking chair ever since Ida and Hartland found him in the henhouse with the dead rooster. Not long afterward Ida noticed Hartland was having trouble talking. He would jabber faster and faster, scrambling to keep up with his racing mind and tangling words and sentence-scraps into snarled heaps. The teasing of his schoolmates, along with the wheezing attacks caused by his asthma, eventually trained him to speak only in cases of urgency. Whenever Warren had something to say, which was about once a month, 'little' came out like 'widow,' 'racoon' like 'waccoon.' And their daughter — Warren and Ida's daughter— was mute.

Sarah did not giggle when tickled, she did not sing. Ida worried the girl would get caught somewhere on the farm — under an abandoned piece of machinery or in a hole in the ground — and be unable to yell for help. Unable or unwilling. The doctor, after examining her tongue, teeth, vocal cords, the roof of her mouth, had said she was capable of speech and would likely start to talk when she found it necessary.

Ida wiped her husband's mouth with a facecloth and went to the kitchen. A woman Ida had met with a whole family of children like Sarah had once recommended 'television therapy' for the girl. Warren had the TV on constantly now that they had the new antenna. It hadn't done anything for Sarah but maybe it was working for James.

*"Mr. President, there's an anecdote you've told time and again about an old football coach from your college days. With the season warming up once again, would you mind repeating it for our viewers?"*

· · ·

The glassy rust ball of the rooster's eye reflected a needle-sharp sun and the spare figure of a man. Hartland Cole's shoulders were stooped and the weight of his lanky frame rested on the balls of his feet as though he were hung over a post by the breastbone. A dozen white hens and the reddy-brown rooster clustered around his snow-covered boots as he stood shivering in the chickencoop doorway. The rooster eyed the pail in Hartland's hand. Hartland rubbed the knuckles of his gloves together. The snowglare of

89

winter sunlight burned his eyes. Finally the bird stepped outside by a small tarpaper-lined bin and pecked at the eggshell in the snow.

Hartland glanced at the housetrailer then ducked back quickly. Slowly he peeked round the corner with one eye as his mother's head and shoulders filled the kitchen window. The new TV satellite dish, pointed to the sun, shaded the southwest corner of the trailer. Hartland's chest wheezed above the henhouse din as he stood and spied on his mother while she washed dishes.

"Maybe you think it'll go unnoticed," he muttered in a voice that was all nose. His wheezing increased in speed then subsided.

He stepped out of the chickencoop, nearly trampling the red rooster with his long feet. He flapped open the springy lid of the feedbin and scooped out a pailful of wheat. Tough bungs of twisted steel wool choked rat-gnawed holes in the plywood sides of the box. The gabbling birds hushed when he dumped the grain into the feedtrough then fluttered as he walloped the pail against a snowshovel to loosen a cake of rotten wheat.

On his way to the barn he passed a smouldering barrel. The fire's heat soothed a dull ache in his ears. He moved closer to the barrel and looked inside. Frantically he looked around until he found a short branch leaning against the chickenfence. He speared into the barrel and flung out a charred snowshoe reeking of burnt babiche. "That asshole Warren!" He poked the branch into the webbed pouch of a lacrosse stick and tossed it on the ground. Unless it was an early type of fishnet he had no idea of its original purpose. What he did know was that it had belonged to his father like the other articles in the barrel. He hauled out the remains of a second snowshoe, some rusty skates and square brown hockey kneepads, a pair of skis and a smoking canoe paddle, and left them to cool in the snow.

"Maybe you think so," he muttered.

At the barn he filled two five-gallon pails with a mush of vegetable slops and spoiled grain. He carried the swill to feed the pigs and had just filled the last trough when he heard the porch door slam. Through the barn doorway he saw Warren Putnam walk out into the snow wearing open galoshes, greasy trousers and a whitish undershirt. Warren opened the door of his station wagon, sat inside for a few seconds and came out with a lit cigarette in his mouth. Hartland watched him stomp up the steps and go back into the trailer.

"Maybe you think it won't be accounted for," he said, the wheezing starting up again.

Hartland climbed the ladder to the hayloft and kicked a couple of bales through a rectangular hole in the floor then dropped himself down, yanked on the twine binding loops to spring open the bales and carried armfuls of coarse slough-hay to the stalls of the cow, the pet goat and the mule. He climbed again to the loft and entered an unused stall.

Atop the trunk Hartland's grandfather had wagoned from Ontario were a canvas tarpaulin, the bones of a saddle and an ancient washbucket full

90

of old blue and green jars. He quickly peeled back the tarp, moved aside the junk, and opened the trunk. A portrait of King George in military uniform, a sour-smelling sheaf of blotty old letters, and a black metal box lay in a neat stack. Hartland leafed through the wad of his own secret papers inside the box for a clipping from the previous month's *Midwest Monthly*: a letter column entitled, 'Wake Up, America!' by a thirteen-year-old prodigy preacher named Little Dothan.

Dear Buffaloed in B.P.,

Your father's problem is a common one in our times. The emptiness in his eyes indicates an absence of spirit. Satan has stolen into your father and simply snatched him away, leaving only the earthly shell which we all know to be nothing more than a vulgar mask over the soul. Only the hand of God can save your father. But don't despair, I will be in your town soon and together we'll "beat the devil out of him!"

A photograph at the top of the advice column showed a bright-eyed, smiling boy with full healthy cheeks. The evangelist's signature flowed confidently across the botom of the picture, a dashing fanfare swooping back over 't"s and 'i' in a spirited flourish.

"Hartland," his mother's voice called faintly. He wheezed a few times, took a long breath of the musty barn air and stuffed the clipping in his shirt pocket. He stowed the tin box and went and peeped through the bottom corner of the high diamond-shaped window.

"Hartland. Are you coming?" His mother stood a few seconds in front of the porch step then began walking toward the valley road by the river. The truck was always parked on a hillside because the battery was dead. Once it was rolling it could be started by popping the clutch.

Hartland stood on tiptoe and pointed a bony finger. He aligned his sharp nose with his finger and followed his mother as she climbed into the cab and clanged the door. "Maybe — you — think," he bit off each word, "that the sins you commit in this world don't get paid for in the next." The green pickup came rolling down the shaded valley hillside and over the small bridge, a great cloud of blue smoke coughing from the tailpipe just before his mother turned in the yard gate. Hartland left his perch and clambered down the gaunt ladder two rungs at a time.

Jaws clenched, eyebrows curved like the horns of a wild steer, Hartland saw himself dressed in a broad-brimmed black hat and long black coat as he strode fiercely toward the trailer until, spotting his mother get out of the idling truck, he stopped and stood, feet set wide, hands on hips, eyeing her. "Maybe you think..." he murmured. When his mother looked his way and waved, he trod on, cutting a straight path in the snow until he was looming, wheezing, before her, close enough to bite the top of her

DANIEL MCBAIN

head. She had begun to scrape the frosty windshield with a stainless steel egglifter.

"Why don't you come into Buffalo Plains?" she said, shading her eyes as she turned halfway toward Hartland. The porch door closed and Hartland's half-sister Sarah came down the steps, dressed to go to town. "You never know, this fair might be really—"

"Maybe," he elbowed in, "m-maybe you th-th-th, m-m-m—aybe you th-think that, you-you th-th-m-m-maymm..." He broke off, wheezing so hard he had to lean over the hood of the truck and breathe. He began to cough hoarsely.

"Sarah go get Hartland's inhaler," said his mother, but the little blonde girl was already halfway up the steps. In an instant she was back with a plastic pump. Hartland inhaled twice on it. His face was drawn and his eyes glassy. He slowly caught his breath.

"Rest for a little while," said his mother. "Take Warren's car if you decide to come."

Hartland nodded and turned wearily toward the house.

Inside the porch Hartland unzipped his overalls and hung them over a pair of deer antlers mounted on the wall, then climbed into a navy blue skidoo-suit, pulled a green facemask toque over his sandy hair and rolled the mask up over his forehead. He searched through the pockets of Warren Putnam's jacket for his car keys but found only empty matchbooks, soft as flannel. Other sets of keys were hooked into the wire cage of a dartboard hung on the porch wall, but not Warren's. Across from his father's Winnipeg couch in the sunny kitchen he checked the table, the counter, the lost world of coupons and clothespins, epoxy glue and lock de-icer in the kitchen junk drawer.

Warren's car was a faded blue station wagon littered with *du Maurier* cigarette packs, sunflower seed shells, Molson beercaps, the greasy stem of a hydraulic jack. In the back was a mould-blue foam mattress and in the corner of the rear window, hiding a faded CKRM sticker, an orange plastic hand that waved side-to-side on a stiff wire when the car was in motion. Hartland knew Warren would allow him to use it if he asked but he didn't want to ask.

*"But Looo-see, we're all gonna be rich! Deese tine I got a fold-proof plan."*

*"I think you mean a fool-proof plan."*

*"No, I mean fold-proof. Look!"*

James Cole sat in the living room, staring, the gray army blanket over his lap as it had been most of Hartland's life. Hartland tiptoed gingerly past his father's rocker to the chesterfield where Warren's soft snoring body formed a sloppy 'S'. On the floor next to the couch lay James' old gray dog Pogey, who had gone unnamed until Warren arrived and gave him a name that stuck. Warren's hair was darkened to an oily crow colour from need of

92

washing.  Bits of lint stuck to his black whiskers.  His undershirt had ridden partway up his back, exposing a bulge of pink flesh.  The crack of his buttocks peered sadly over his belt.

Hartland lightly patted Warren's left pocket.  No keys.  He craned over the greasy body to see his other pocket but it was buried under the long sausage of Warren's right thigh.  His eyes darted about the room as he wondered where else Warren might have left them.  They might be in his mother's bedroom, he thought, but he disliked going in there and having to look at Warren's dirty clothes draped over a chair, Warren's cigarette butts in the night table ashtray.

Hartland glanced at the blue picture on the television screen.  *King Kong is clinging fiercely to the Statue of Liberty, a buxom blonde in his hand.  Distressed, the woman shakes a box of 'Poppervescent' candies into his mouth.  Kong's eyes swirl in their sockets as the screen explodes in sparkles, accompanied by a fizzing sound.  "Popp-pervescents..." whispers a chorus of sexy female voices.  In the next shot Kong is lying passively beneath a palm tree with the blonde, who continues dropping candies in his mouth.  His eyes spin and his head sizzles.  The camera dissolves from the tropical island to a box of Poppervescents held in the Statue of Liberty's hand.*

"Profligacy," said Hartland under his breath.  He changed channels.

*"Under no circumstances will this administration tolerate the presence of another government in this hemisphere falling into the clutches of the Soviets."*

Warren's snoring died with a gulp and he rolled onto his left side, bouncing heavily like a rocking bobsled and sliding the cushion another inch from the back of the couch.  Harland stood motionless until the groaning rhythm recommenced.  He gently patted Warren's right pocket.  No keys.

He spun around.  His father had stopped rocking and was staring at the television set.  Immediately he started to rock again and his eyes went blank like they always were.  Hartland decided he'd imagined it.

Then he spotted the keychain lying behind Warren's rump, a brown leather flap with a silver medallion inscribed, "DART PLAYERS DO IT WITH THEIR POINTY PARTS."  He reached into the split between the two olive-green cushions and he snapped up the keys as well as a penny, two quarters and a nickel.

Next he turned to his father.  Hartland jumped.  His father was leaning forward in his rocker, pointing to the TV screen where a microwave oven was being displayed.  Then the man resumed rocking like usual.  Must be the inhaler making me see things, he thought.  He gripped his father by the shoulders and hoisted him to his feet.  The rocking chair rocked to a stop.  Disregarding the crumpled flannel that clotted up at the joints, he stuffed his father's pyjama-clad legs into a pair of trousers and pushed his

93

arms through the sleeves of a woolen sweater. He swathed the man in the gray blanket, eased him onto his shoulder and slowly stood erect.

It occurred to Hartland that Warren's snoring had again ceased. He turned, his swaddled father slung over his shoulder, to see two dewy blue eyes peeking through the creases of Warren's puffed eyelids.

"What ow you up to?" Warren's speech had a childish, sponge-mouthed quality that made him sound like a cartoon character.

Hartland's neck muscles tensed and his face grew hot. His eyes burned into Warren's as he struggled to keep his breath regular. "I'm up to g-g-gettin' a man his soul b-b—back!" he blurted, each breath a slight rasp.

Warren made a farting noise with his lips.

BRIAN BARTLETT will have a short story in the anthology of Quebec fiction published by Cormorant this fall. He has published poems in *Prism, Queen's Quarterly, The Canadian Forum* and *Rubicon.*

HENRY BEISSEL, poet, playwright, translator and editor, was born in Cologne, Germany in 1929 and came to Canada in 1951. His most recent publications include two of his plays, *The Noose* and *Mr. X* (Cormorant Books) and *Poems, New and Collected* (Mosaic Press).

ANN CIMON is a Montreal poet and free-lance book reviewer. She has published a book of poems and prose entitled *A Skin of Snow.*

LEONARD COHEN's last collection of poems, *Book of Mercy* was published by McClelland and Stewart in 1984.

SU CROLL is a Concordia University creative writing student. Her work appears in the Nu-Age anthology, *Passions and Poisons.*

LORNA CROZIER's latest collection, *The Garden Going on Without Us* was shortlisted for the 1986 Governor General's award for poetry.

ANN DIAMOND, the former Anne Mclean, was born in Montreal. She writes poetry and fiction. Her most recent publication is *A Nun's Diary* (Signal Editions of Vehicle Press) which was nominated for the Canadian Author's Award in 1985.

PEGGY HOFFMAN is a creative writing teacher at Bialik High School in Montreal.

ALEXANDER HUTCHISON is a Scottish poet who has spent considerable time in Canada. He is the author of several collections of poems, including *Deep Tap Tree* and *Mr. Scales at the Auction,* and editor of the audio cassette magazine *Bonfire.* He lives in Edinburgh.

W.P. KINSELLA is the author of twelve books. He has had over two hundred stories published in magazines and journals world-wide. His most recent books are *The Alligator Report, The Iowa Baseball Conspiracy,* and *The Fencepost Chronicles.*

IRVING LAYTON's latest book of poems is *Final Reckoning: Poems 1982-86* (Mosaic Press). His *Selected Letters,* edited by Francis Manbridge, will be published in the fall by the University of British Columbia Press.

SERVANDO MACBANUA is a New People's Army guerilla fighter in the Philippines.

EDGAR MARANAN won the 2nd Prize for poetry in the Carlos Palanca Memorial Awards for literature for his anthology, *Foliage and Tiger Fire and Other Poems*. He is a former instructor of political science at the University of the Philippines.

DANIEL MCBAIN was born in southern Saskatchewan. He is a graduate of the creative writing program of Concordia University, and has published short fiction in several journals including *Pegasus, X-it: The Magazine of Contemporary Thought and Blue Buffalo*. His selection in the anthology is part of a longer work.

SHIE MIN is a Chinese playwright, born in 1934. His works have been produced in China, Roumania and Yugoslavia.

JENNIFER MITTON has recently returned from a two-year CUSO teaching position in Nigeria. She is presently in the creative writing program at U.B.C. and Fiction Editor of *Prism International*.

MARTIN MOONEY lives in Belfast. He has been recognized in *Trio*, an annual anthology which showcases new talent from Northern Ireland. He is 25.

SHERYL L. NELMS is from Marysville, Kansas. Her work has appeared in several magazines, and her book of poems, *Their Combs Turn Red in the Spring*, is available from Northwoods Press.

NJABULO S. NDEBELE's *Fools and other stories* (Readers International) won the Noma Award for the best book published in Africa in 1984. His poetry, fiction and critical essays have appeared in his native South Africa and abroad. He is head of the department of English at the University of Lesotho and is currently working on a novel.

JIA-LIN PENG, a fiction writer and translator, was born in 1948. He is presently in Canada on a fellowship to complete his M.A. in English Literature at Concordia University.

JOSE MARIA SISON is the founder of the new communist party of the Philippines. He was a graduate student at the University of Manila and published a collection of poems entitled *Brothers*. He is also the author of *Philippine Society and Revolution*.

TODD SWIFT is 21. He is presently arranging an exchange anthology of new Northern Irish and Canadian poets, including Martin Mooney.

HOWARD TESSLER is a native Montreal writer and film-maker. His chap-book, *Saturday Night at the Ritz*, was recently published by Brandon University.